BRITISH PIONEERS IN CALIFORNIA

A Thesis

by

Douglas H. Maynard

OCCIDENTAL COLLEGE

1948

583766

Reprinted in 1974 by

R AND E RESEARCH ASSOCIATES
4843 Mission Street, San Francisco   94112
18581 McFarland Avenue, Saratoga, California   95070

PUBLISHERS AND DISTRIBUTORS OF ETHNIC STUDIES

Editor: Adam S. Eterovich
Publisher: Robert D. Reed

LIBRARY OF CONGRESS CARD CATALOG NUMBER

74-76671

ISBN
0-88247-261-5

TABLE OF CONTENTS

PREFACE

The history of the United States is in large part a reflection of European politics and European life. It is unnecessary to restate the fact that Europe gave to the United States its white population, its language, many of its customs, its literary tradition, its religion, and the basis of its political heritage. European politics and European life also directly influenced the history of early California, which until the middle of the nineteenth century was far removed from the United States. In some respects California on the Pacific Coast resembles the older American states on the Atlantic Coast. In spite of the obvious dissimilarities between the two regions in matters of settlement, climate, chronology, and political development, both seaboards were objects of European colonial rivalry, both felt direct European impress, and both fell under Anglo-Saxon domination.

The early settlement of California is one small segment of the European conquest of North America. The participation of the British in the development of eastern America forms a large part of the history of the United States, but their activities on the West Coast, when California was ruled by Spain and Mexico, have been neglected. In the hope of removing some of the obscurity surrounding this phase of American history the following study has been undertaken.

I wish to express my gratitude to Dr. Robert Glass Cleland, Dr. Glenn Dumke, and Dr. Osgood Hardy of the Department of History of Occidental College for the advice, criticism, and aid which they have given me. I also wish to acknowledge my debt to the reference librarians of the Occidental College Library, the University of California at Los Angeles Library, the Los Angeles Public Library, the Pasadena Public Library, and the Henry E. Huntington Library.

INTRODUCTION

This is a study of the British pioneers who came to California during the time that this province was ruled by Spain and Mexico. A goodly proportion of the foreign-born residents of early California were of British birth. Many other nationalities, including French, German and American, were represented in lesser numbers, until in the 1840's the last named group was to grow quickly in size, surpassing the other foreign segments and in 1846 overwhelming the native inhabitants.

For several reasons the story is concluded with the American conquest. In the first place, the annexation of California by the United States ended the province's long and perilous career as a poorly chaperoned and at the same time desirable section of the New World. Once union to the United States had been sanctified by the Treaty of Guadalupe Hidalgo, no longer was there opportunity for international coquetry, and romantic, exotic California settled down to a prosaic and Americanized life. Plots of European nationals, including Englishmen, to raise their native flags over California ceased as the possibility of the province's return to a colonial status was ended.

The American conquest was chosen as a terminal date, secondly, because this event took place almost simultaneously with the discovery of gold. For a few brief years California celebrated its inclusion in the United States in riotous, Gold Rush living before accepting the responsibilities of an American state. The Gold Rush witnessed the arrival of gold seekers from all parts of the world. The role played by Englishmen in the frenzied migration to California and their activities in the gold fields offers material for a separate study and for that reason is not included.

Thirdly, the British immigrants who came to California after this period found a predominantly Anglo-Saxon society which quickly engulfed them in its swelling population.

It is necessary, now that a final date has been established, to indicate the point at which the narrative begins. Strictly speaking, a study of British pioneers in California need go back no further than the year 1814, for it was at that time that the first British citizen to become a permanent resident disembarked in Alta California. However, for the purpose of clarity and inclusiveness, the British interest in California is traced back to its beginning with Drake's "Famous Voyage," and the struggle waged by the outside world against the commercial and residential monopoly which Spain subsequently established in California is considered.

The victory of the foreigners in this contest resulted in a slow but steady trickle of non-Spanish immigration, in which the Britishers were at once prominent. Although of a limited number, many of them rose to positions of respect and influence in the community. They served in various capacities -- from artisans to professional men -- and in general were of benefit to the region. But they and their American counterparts were to hasten the end of California as a dreamy, picturesque, backward -- yet happy -- Mexican state.

Although the British residents were personally respected by their fellow citizens, it was feared that they wished to see California taken under the protection of the British empire. The decades of the 1830's and the 1840's saw numerous plans for the alienation of California from Mexican rule when it became apparent that Mexico could not effectively maintain political control over that region. These plans were developed inside the province and without. The most aggressive plotters were the citizens of the United States, whose desires for territorial expansion were embodied in "manifest destiny" -- the belief that the United States was bound to sweep from coast to coast, if not from polar regions to the Panamanian isthmus. Their aggressive designs quite naturally prompted a suspicion that other nations had similar intentions. The result was that American residents living in California and expansionists in the United States believed that Great Britain was threatening to seize the land on which they had set their hearts, and they urged action to forestall such a development. For many years after the American conquest it was felt that only the American seizure of California had prevented it from being acquired by perfidious Albion. This significant phase of Anglo-California relations will be considered in Chapter IV, in which it becomes apparent that although various Englishmen advocated the acquisition of California, the administration in London was cool to the proposal and that the province was in little danger of falling into British hands.

The California of 1948 bears little resemblance to the territory of one hundred years ago. The British pioneers and the golden era in which they participated have now, in one brief century, been relegated to the dim, distant and almost unbelievable past. Only a few crumbling missions, occasional, inconspicuous names -- a Dalton Canyon, a Hartnell Street, a Richardson's Bay -- give evidence of a former civilization and the extranjeros who had participated in it. But in these brief symbols are represented in a microcosm the expansion of empires and the history of the New World.

CHAPTER I

GREAT BRITAIN AND CALIFORNIA

1. DRAKE'S "FAMOUS VOYAGE"

The relationship between England and California has a long and colorful history. From the time that Sir Francis Drake landed in California, until that province was finally annexed by the United States, Englishmen played a conspicuous role in its development. The colonization of California in 1769 was prompted, in large measure, by fear of English aggression along the Pacific Coast. The establishment of a post at Monterey was also encouraged to provide a refuge from the English freebooters for the Manila galleon. After its settlement, California seethed with rumors of English encroachment up until the time that a more aggressive neighbor was to replace England as the greatest threat to Spanish and to Mexican sovereignty.

Anglo-California relations had an impressive beginning, for it was the most famous of English navigators, Sir Francis Drake, who first brought California within the scope of English knowledge by leading to its shores the second European expedition to reach this area. In the year 1577, Drake, in command of an expedition of five small ships, set out from England on a voyage that was eventually to lead around the world and to become one of the most famous voyages of history.[1] The expedition had several purposes. They included: (1) injuring the Spanish Empire by raiding its treasure ships and plundering its cities on the Pacific,[2] (2) acquiring gold, silver, and other precious goods thereby, (3) planting a small English colony in the New World, and (4) searching for the Northwest Passage.[3] One writer believes that Drake's backers were primarily interested in establishing trade with the Spice Islands,[4] but the freebooting purpose was undoubtedly uppermost in Drake's own mind.

The fleet proceeded via the Strait of Magellan to the Pacific Ocean where it was met by a terrific storm. The ships were separated, and only the flagship, the Golden Hind, continued the voyage. Cruising up the Pacific Coast of South America, Drake was spectacularly successful in plundering the surprised Spaniards, who had not anticipated hostile attacks in this part of the world.

---

1. Francis Drake, The World Encompassed by Sir Francis Drake (London, 1854), pp. 6-7.
2. John W. Robertson, Francis Drake and Other Early Explorers Along the Pacific Coast (San Francisco, 1927), p. 89.
3. Robert Glass Cleland, Pathfinders (Los Angeles, 1929), p. 27.
4. Henry R. Wagner, Sir Francis Drake's Voyage Around the World (San Francisco, 1926), pp. 26-27.

After accumulating a vast amount of treasure, Drake was faced with the problem of choosing a route back to England. The idea of returning by way of the Strait of Magellan was discarded because of the natural dangers of that route and because the Spaniards would probably be waiting for him at the tip of South America.[5] Another alternative was to cross the Pacific and reach England via the Cape of Good Hope. A third possibility was the long sought for Strait of Anian, north of the American continents.

If the season had not been so far advanced, Drake perhaps would have taken the course of the eastbound galleon and sailed directly from the Mexican coast to the Moluccas. But since the crossing of the Pacific could not be begun with safety for some months, Drake occupied the intervening time by making a long voyage to the northwest, presumably looking for the Pacific entrance to the Northwest Passage or even searching for the Kingdom of the Gran Quivira, so much in vogue among the Spaniards.[6]

Sailing northward from April 16, 1579 to June 5, 1579, Drake was eventually forced to turn back because of the cold.[7] The _Golden Hind_ then proceeded to the southward "...til we came within thirtie eight degrees towardes the line, in which height it pleased God to send us into a faire and good bay, with a good winde to enter the same."[8] The ship anchored on the 17th of June and remained there until July 23.

Our Generall called the country Nova Albion, and that for two causes: the one in respect of the white bankes and cliffes, which lie towards the sea: and the other, because it might have some affinitie with our country in name, which sometime was so called.[9]

A controversy has raged for many years as to which bay Drake actually visited: some authorities believe it was Drake's Bay, others Trinidad and Bodega Bays.[10]

The Indians showed little fear of the Englishmen, and Drake treated them kindly, exchanging presents with them and giving them clothes "to

---

5. Richard Hakluyt, _The Voyages of the English Nation to America_ (4 vol., Edinburgh, 1890), IV, 40-41.
6. Robert Glass Cleland, _From Wilderness to Empire: A History of California, 1542-1900_ (New York, 1944), p. 21.
7. Just how far north he actually sailed has been a topic of discussion for many years. The latitude was given as 48° N. in Drake, _op. cit._, p. 115 and 43° N. in Hakluyt, _op. cit._, IV, 41.
8. Hakluyt, _op. cit._, IV, 41.
9. _Ibid._, IV, 44-45
10. Wagner, _op. cit._, p. 154-169.

cover their nakedness." As the ship had developed a leak which needed repairing, it was brought in near to the shore and unloaded, and a stone fort was erected to protect the supplies and the crew while repairs were effected.

The Indians came to look upon the newcomers as gods. Although the sailors did their best to discourage this belief, they were unsuccessful, and the Indians insisted upon mutilating themselves before the white man. Every three days the natives brought presents of food and tobacco. The friendly reception was climaxed several days later by a ceremony in which, the Englishmen believed, sovereignty over the land was conferred upon Drake.

> When they had satisfied themselves, they made signes to our
> Generall to sit downe, to whom the king, and diuers others made
> seuerall orations, or rather supplications, that he would take
> their king, making signes that they would resigne unto him
> their right and title of the whole land, and become his subjects.
> In which to perswade vs the better, the king and the rest, with
> one consent and with great reuerence joyfully singing a song did
> set the crowne vpon his head, inriching his necke with all their
> chaines, and offered vnto him many other things, honouring him
> by the name of Hioh, adding thereunto as it seemed a signe of
> triumph; which thing our Generall thought not meete to reiect
> because hee knewe not what honour and profite it might bee to
> our countrey. Wherefore in the name, and to the vse of her
> Maiestie, he tooke the scepter, crowne and digntie of the said
> countrey in his hands, wishing that the riches and treasure
> thereof might so conueniently be transported to the inriching of
> her kingdome at home, as it aboundeth in the same.[11]

While on the coast Drake and a few of his companions travelled in-land to visit some of the Indian villages. They found the countryside there to be "...farre different from the shoare, a goodly country, and fruitful soyle, stored with many blessings fit for the vse of men." They came across herds of deer "...being most large and fat of body", and many small animals which they called "conies." These gopher-like animals were eaten by the Indians, and their skins were used for clothing. The Englishmen reached the conclusion that the possibilities of finding gold and silver in that region were promising.

Finally Drake made preparations to leave, much to the distress of the natives. Having received the surrounding area from the inhabitants, Drake determined to lay formal claim to it. It was believed that the Spanish had not visited that region nor discovered "...the land by many

---

11. Hakluyt, op. cit., IV, 43-44.

degrees to the southward of this place."[12] According to the narrator:

> At our departure hence our Generall set vp a monument of our
> being there; as also of her Maiesties right and title to the
> same, namely a plate nailed vpon a faire great poste, where-
> upon was ingrauen her Maiesties name, the day and years of
> our arriual there, with the free giuing vp of the prouince
> and people into her Maiesties hands, together with her high-
> ness picture and armes, in a piece of sixe pence of current
> English money vnder the plate, where vnder was also written
> the name of our Generall.[13]

It is interesting to note that in 1936 a plate, believed to be the
one left by Drake, was discovered in Marin County near San Rafael. The
inscription reads:

> Bee It Knowne Vnto All Men By These Presents
>   IVNE 17 1579
> By The Grace Of God And In The Name Of Herr Maiesty Qveen
> Elizabeth Of England And Herr Successors Forever I Take
> Possession Of This Kingdome Whose King And People Freely
> Resigne Their Right And Title In The Whole And Vnto Herr
> Maiesties Keeping Now Named By Me An To Bee Known Vnto All
> Men As Nova Albion.
>
>   Francis Drake[14]

The Golden Hind sailed on July 23, 1579 and was off the Farrallon
Islands (which Drake called the Islands of Saint James) the following
day. Inasmuch as the weather continued to be cold, and "...the wind
blowing still (as it did at first) from the northwest, cut off all hope
of finding a passage through these northerne parts,"[15] Drake set his
course for the Molucca Islands. Continuing on around the Cape of Good
Hope, he reached England on September 26, 1580.

As stated above, one of the purposes of Drake's expedition was to
establish an English colony in the New World. It appears that California may have been the region selected. In the first place the name,
Nova Albion, which Drake conferred upon this region "...that it might
have some affinitie, euen in name also, with our own country," suggests
that it was to be the basis of an English colony in America, as was New
Spain for England's powerful rival. Secondly, Drake believed, erroneously,
that the Spaniards had not progressed as far north as Nova Albion, thus
leaving it as unclaimed territory. In his generous treatment of the

---

12. Ibid., IV, 45.
13. Ibid.
14. Herbert E. Bolton, Drake's Plate of Brass Evidence of His
Visit to California in 1579 (San Francisco, 1937), p. 11.
15. Drake, op.cit., p. 134.

4

natives, it might appear that Drake was laying the foundations for peaceful relations with them if a colony should be established. Moreover, Nova Albion was found to be a land worth colonizing, "...a goodly country... stored with many blessings fit of the vse of man." It was also observed that "...there is no part of the earth here to be taken up, wherein there is not some special likelihood of gold or silver."

A document, which some authorities regard as evidence that Drake intended to establish an English empire in California, is a sixteenth century map showing Drake's "Famous Voyage."[16] The map bears the inscription, "Carte venee corige par le dict Siegneur droch": "Map seen and corrected by the said Sir Drake." The crown and arms of the Queen are inscribed on the northwest coast of North America, and a boundary line separating "Nova Albion" from "Nova Hispanie" has been drawn from the Gulf of California to the point at which the Mississippi River flows into the Gulf of Mexico. All of North America above that line is represented as part of "Nova Albion" except for a small triangle marked "Nova France" on the east coast of North America.

Soon after his return to England, Drake was issued a royal charter, providing for the organization of a company to establish a colony in the New World.[17] Although the location of the proposed colony is not stated, in all probability it was California.[18] There is also evidence that Drake planned another expedition soon after his return. A letter from the Spanish ambassador in London to Phillip II, dated January 9, 1581, states that the Queen had authorized Drake to lead an expedition of ten ships "for the Moluccas" and that a second group of six ships was to go to Brazil and join Drake later. Because of the imminence of war, and other political complications, the plan had to be abandoned.[19] Another expedition was sent out, but it failed to accomplish its purpose. "Thus the attempt to colonize New Albion and establish trade relations with the East Indies was frustrated."[20]

In spite of this fact, Drake's voyage had several indirect effects on California. It demonstrated the vulnerability of Spanish shipping and Spanish settlements in the Pacific area, and it tempted other freebooters to follow his example in raiding them. It brought home to the Spaniards the danger of foreign aggression in this area and stimulated efforts which were eventually to lead to the occupation of California. The voyage also helped to precipitate war between Spain and England.[21]

---

16. New Light on Drake: A Collection of Documents Relating to His Voyage of Circumnavigation 1577-1580 (Tr. ed. by Mrs. Lelia Nuttall) (London, 1914), pp. liv-lvi.
17. Nuttall, op. cit., p. 430
18. Charles E. Chapman, A History of California, The Spanish Period (New York, 1921), p. 109.
19. Nuttall, op. cit., p. xxxviii.
20. Ibid., p. xxxix.
21. Cleland, Wilderness to Empire, p. 24.

2. THE ENGLISH APPROACH TO THE PACIFIC OCEAN

After Drake's plan to colonize Nova Albion failed (if the assumption that he had such a plan is correct), it was to be more than two centuries before any Englishman was again to set foot in California. However, the English were gradually extending their activities in that direction. The first of several avenues of approach to the Pacific was the Isthmus of Panama. Drake and Hawkins had at one time used that route, and later pirates, typified by Sir Henry Morgan, were to center their activities there.[22] A second line of advance was around Africa to southern Asia. Although most of the energy expended in this direction was required to battle the Portuguese, Dutch, and French in India, the capture of Manila in 1762 by an English expedition from India gave just cause for alarm.[23]

There was also the English overland advance across the American continent. In the north the Hudson's Bay Company was gradually working its way westward. At the time of the founding of California, this approach represented only a potential threat as the trappers were still far in the interior. Further south another type of advance had begun -- a westward movement of settlers from the Atlantic Coast, which becoming American instead of English in 1776, was to prove the most serious threat to California.

However, in the years preceding Spain's settlement of California, the most menacing avenue of English approach was around Cape Horn and up the broad Pacific. The route which Drake had followed was later used by other English and Dutch freebooters, and in the years 1740-1744 Anson lead a formal naval expedition to the Pacific by this route. After the Seven Years War, Englishmen came on scientific-exploratory expeditions rather than as buccaneers.

3. THE SEA OTTER TRADE

a. CAPTAIN COOK'S THIRD VOYAGE

The most famous of the later explorers was Captain James Cook, who commanded three epoch-making expeditions to the Pacific. The third voyage was of greatest significance to California, although it did not include a visit to that province, because it was primarily responsible for establishing the sea otter trade in America.

The "Secret Instructions" issued to Cook "by the Commissioners for Executing the Office of Lord High Admiral of Great Britain and Ireland," gave as the purpose of the voyage the discovery of a northern passage from the Pacific to the Atlantic Ocean. He was instructed to leave the

---

22. Chapman, The Spanish Period, p. 260.
23. Ibid., pp. 260-261.

Society Islands in the beginning of February, 1778, and to approach Nova Albion in latitude 45° N. From that point he was to sail up the coast in search of the Northwest Passage. Cook was "...strictly enjoined not to touch upon any part of the Spanish dominions on the western continent of America, unless driven thither by some unavoidable accident."[24]

It is interesting to note that Neve, Governor of California, had orders from Spain to be on the lookout for Captain Cook's two vessels and by no means to permit them to enter any California port.[25] However, during the hostilities of the American Revolutionary War, Spain, as well as France and the United States, issued orders to her fleet not to interfere with Cook's expedition.[26]

Cook left England on July 17, 1776, in the _Resolution_, which was accompanied by the _Discovery_. Proceeding via Cape Hope, Tasmania, New Zealand, the Society Islands, and the Sandwich Islands (which were discovered and named at this time), Cook reached the coast of New Albion in the vicinity of 44° 33' N on March 6, 1778.[27] He then sailed northward, examining the coast line for indications of a through passageway. On March 29, 1778, Cook anchored in a bay, which he named King George's Sound, before discovering that the inhabitants called it Nootka. The natives offered to sell various furs "...in particular, of the sea otter." For the furs Cook's officers and men exchanged knives, chisels, nails, looking glasses, etc. Said Cook of the sea otter:

> The fur of these animals.......is certainly softer and finer
> than that of any others we know of; and therefore the dis-
> covery of this part of the continent of North America, where
> so valuable an article of commerce may be met with, cannot
> be a matter of indifference.[28]

After proceeding through Bering Strait, Cook reached 70° 44'N before he was turned back by ice and the approach of winter. He returned to the Sandwich Islands to spend the winter and was killed there in a skirmish with the natives on February 14, 1779. Charles Clerke, Captain of the _Discovery_, succeeded to command and resumed the search for a northern passage that spring. His health undermined by the rigours of the cruise, Clerke died on August 22, 1779, and he was, in turn, succeeded by John Gore. Because of the poor condition of the ships and the lack of supplies, the expedition headed homeward.

---

24. James Cook, The Three Voyages of Captain James Cook Round the World (7 vols., London, 1821), V. 33.

25. Hubert Howe Bancroft, History of California (7 vols., San Francisco, 1884-1890), I, 309-310.

26. J. C. Beaglehole, The Exploration of the Pacific (London, 1934), p. 349.

27. The Oregon-California border is 42° N.

28. Cook, op. cit., VII, 335.

In Siberia, where a brief stop was made for repairs, the Russians bought a few of the sea otter furs for prices ranging upward to thirty ruples.[29] Continuing the voyage, the two ships anchored at Macao, China on December 1, 1779. At that port Cook's men found a good market for their otter pelts, where some of the better ones were sold for as much as $120.00. The furs had been collected without any idea of their value, and many had been worn by the Indians before their purchase. The sailors used them for bed clothers and for other purposes, but even in their worn condition they were hastily bought by the Chinese.

The sailors benefited so much from these transactions that they were eager to make another trip to the Northwest Coast.

> The rage with which our seamen were possessed to return to Cook's River and by (sic) another cargo of skins to make their fortune at one time, was not far short of mutiny...[30]

However, Gore directed the ships towards home, and they anchored off the Nore on October 4, 1780.

b. THE NOOTKA SOUND CONTROVERSY

Sailing to the Northwest Coast, other English ships soon followed up the opportunities for trade that were thus discovered. The activities of the sea otter hunters brought England and Spain close to war in the so-called "Nootka Sound Controversy". As a result of this international incident, in which Spain came out second best, her policy in the area of North America was changed from the "offensive defensive" to the "defensive defensive",[31] and from the seventeen-nineties on, she tried only to hold on to the territory which had already been won.

The controversy resulted from completely independent attempts by Spain and England (or their nationals), to found settlements in Nootka Sound at the same time. In 1778, Estevan Jose Martinez, the Spanish naval commander on the Pacific coast of North America, had completed a voyage to Alaska to investigate the Russian settlements there. He had become alarmed at the prospect of the Russians erecting a post at Nootka Sound and had obtained permission from the Viceroy to lead an expedition to that region the following year in order to forestall them.

---

29. Cook, op. cit., VII, 335.
30. Ibid., VII, 397.
31. Chapman, <u>The Spanish Period</u>, p. 345. From a defensive policy carried out by offensive means, Spain now promoted her defensive policy by defensive means.

In the summer of 1789 Martinez encountered a British expedition at Nootka Sound which also had plans for founding a settlement there.[32] He captured four British ships, the _Iphigenia_, the _Northwest America_, the _Princess Royal_, and the _Argonaut_. The _Iphigenia_ was freed after an inventory had been taken of her cargo and an agreement signed, by which the owner was to pay the value of the ship and cargo, in case she was judged a good prize. The _Princess Royal_, _Northwest America_, and the _Argonaut_, along with their crews, were sent to New Spain to be acted upon by the Viceroy.

When news of this action reached Europe, a quarrel between England and Spain resulted, which almost ended in war. It became a showdown between the rival colonial claims of England and Spain in North America, and both nations began feverish preparations for the conflict. However, Spain backed down, and England dictated the terms of the treaty signed October 28, 1790. It was agreed that the ships seized were to be restored and reparations paid for the damages inflicted. "The buildings and tracts of land" belonging to the Englishman, Meares, which Martinez had allegedly seized, were to be restored. It was further agreed "... that British subjects shall not navigate or carry on their fishery in the said seas within the distance of 10 maritime leagues from any part of the coast already occupied by Spain."[33] However, Spain agreed to allow other nations to trade north of the occupied portion of the Pacific Coast.

Each country appointed a special commissioner to carry out the restoration of property provided for in the convention. The English selection was Captain George Vancouver.[34] He left England in 1791 with instructions to explore the Northwest Coast, as well as to act as the British commissioner. Arriving at Nootka Sound August, 1792, he met the Spanish representative, Bodega y Cuadro, but the two could not agree on a settlement. Vancouver thought that the whole area should be transferred to the British, while Cuadra held that only the plot of ground on which Meare's building had stood was involved. As a solution, the commissioners agreed to resubmit the case to their respective governments in Europe.

A final agreement was signed at Madrid on January 11, 1794. It provided for the abandonment of the Nootka Sound area by both countries. Although temporary buildings could be erected, no permanent buildings nor fortifications were to be established. A new set of commissioners, Sir Thomas Pierce and Manuel de Alava, met at Nootka on March 23, 1795

---

32. W. R. Manning, "The Nootka Sound Controversy," American Historical Association _Annual Report_ (1904), pp. 303-304.

33. The Nootka Sound Convention cited in Manning, "The Nootka Sound Controversy", _loc. cit._, pp. 454-455.

34. George Vancouver, _A Voyage of Discovery to the Pacific Ocean_, etc. (6 vols., London, 1801), I, 59.

and carried out the agreement.

4.   BRITISH EXPLORERS IN CALIFORNIA

a.   VANCOUVER

George Vancouver, the English commissioner for the execution of the
first Nootka Sound Convention, visited California on three different
occasions. Aside from this political function, an important purpose of
his voyage was the exploration of the coastline of Northwest America.[35]
He was directed to search for a northern passage and to observe the
settlements of European nations on the coast. His was the first of three
official exploring expeditions from Great Britain to visit and report on
California.

In April, 1792, Vancouver's ships, the Discovery and the Chatham,
crossed over from the Sandwich Islands and sailed northward from Cape
Mendocino toward Nootka Sound. After it had been decided to resubmit
the Nootka problem to the English and Spanish governments, Vancouver in
the Discovery sailed southward and anchored in San Francisco Bay on
November 14, 1792. The Englishmen were very well received. Vancouver
and his officers were entertained at the presidio and the mission, and
all the provisions which the region could afford were placed at his
disposal. On November 20 Vancouver and some of his officers, accompanied
by a Spanish military escort, made a trip inland to the Santa Clara
Mission, becoming the first foreigners to penetrate that far into the
countryside.

He was impressed by the mission system and was well pleased with
California in general. However, he noted that although well supplied
with food stuffs, California was deficient in most other types of goods.

Upon his return to San Francisco Bay, he found that the Chatham had
arrived, and preparations were made for getting underway. The commandant would not allow Vancouver to pay for the supplies which the latter
had received but did accept a few presents which Vancouver left. On
November 25 the expedition sailed for Monterey and anchored there the
following day. In Monterey the same cordial reception was extended, and
the month and one-half spent there was filled with parties, picnics,
excursions, firework displays, and other festivities. During that time
the ships were repaired, and water and provisions were taken on board.

When Vancouver prepared to leave, the Spaniards again refused to
accept payment for the cattle and other provisions given to him. He
again resorted to distributing useful articles as gifts. The explorer
had to leave two deserters in the province, but he was loaned the only
Smith in the settlement as a replacement for the lost armorer. He
sailed on January 15, 1793.

---

35. The account of this voyage, except where otherwise indicated,
is taken from Vancouver, op. cit.

Governor Arrillaga, who had been absent from Monterey during this time, was greatly displeased when he learned of the privileges which had been extended to the Englishman. He was especially angry because of Vancouver's trip to Santa Clara and the latter's opportunity to observe the indefensible condition of the country. The commandants of the various presidios were instructed to confine their courtesies in the future to the furnishing of needed supplies.[36]

The Discovery returned to San Francisco on October 19, 1793, and this time she met with a very cool reception. The commandant asked for a formal statement of Vancouver's arrival, his length of stay, and the supplies needed. Vancouver was informed that, except for the purpose of obtaining wood and water, only he and one officer would be allowed to go ashore. He was much offended by this turn of events and sailed for Monterey on October 24.

At the capitol, where he was now dealing with Arrillaga himself, Vancouver met a similar reception. He sailed four days later after taking aboard cattle and other supplies. When the Discovery anchored at Santa Barbara on November 10, the Englishmen were received much more cordially and remained for a pleasant week of recreation. Sailing further down the coast, Vancouver finally left San Diego on December 9 to cruise across the Pacific. He had hoped to receive new instructions on the Nootka question while in California, but in this he had been disappointed.

Vancouver returned to Nootka in September, 1794, hoping that dispatches from England would await him there. As none arrived, he sailed down the coast and anchored at Monterey for the third time on November 7, 1794. Arrillaga had been relieved, and Vancouver received a welcome much more to his liking. His deserters were recovered, the ships were overhauled, and supplies were taken on board. Having learned that a new commissioner had been appointed to execute the second Nootka Sound Convention, he sailed on December 2, 1794, homeward bound.

Vancouver's record of this voyage was published in 1801 in six volumes. A great deal of the record was devoted to California, and it provided the first accurate English description of that province. Aside from the explorer's hostility toward Arrillaga, an interesting and sympathetic account of the new colony is given.

b. BEECHEY

Two other English exploring expeditions were to follow Vancouver to the coast of California. The first was commanded by Captain F. W. Beechey. He left England on May 17, 1825, to rendezvous at Bering

---

36. Bancroft, Calif., I, 514

Strait with expeditions commanded by Captain Parry and Captain Franklin.
The latter expeditions were seeking the Northern Passage, a goal which
had been instrumental in bringing Drake to California two and a half
centuries earlier. Cook and Vancouver had also been dedicated to this
search. In addition to aiding Parry and Franklin,

> As the vessel would traverse in her route, a portion of the
> globe hitherto little explored, and as a considerable
> period must necessarily elapse before her presence would be
> required in the north, it was intended to employ her in
> surveying and exploring such parts of the Pacific as were
> within her reach, and were of the most consequence to
> navigation.[37]

A naturalist, George T. Lay, was added to the ship's complement, and
several of the ship's officers volunteered to perform scientific duties,
besides their regularly assigned ones. In the typical language of navy
officialdom, Beechey was instructed to provide for the collection of
scientific data. "You are to cause it to be understood that two speci-
ments, at least, of each article are to be reserved for the public mus-
eums; afterwhich the naturalist and officers will be at liberty to
collect for themselves."[38]

After spending the summer of 1826 in the area north of Bering Strait,
Beechey was forced to sail southward by the approach of winter. On the
7th of November, 1826, the Blossom entered San Francisco Bay. There
Beechey was hospitably received by Lieutenant Martinez, commandant of the
presidio, and Padre Tomaso of San Francisco Mission. It soon became
evident that San Francisco, aside from providing flour, fresh beef, vegetables, and salt, could not meet all the ships requirements. Consequently, three of the officers were sent overland to Monterey in hopes
of obtaining there the supplies needed. But Monterey did not have the
required medicines and stores, although the purser was able to purchase
some salt meat and a few stores from vessels in the harbor.

In the meantime, the crew was employed in making soundings and sur-
veying the Bay. Martinez cooperated wholeheartedly, asking only a copy
of the chart constructed for his own government. When the three officers
returned from Monterey, Beechey made preparations for getting underway
and sailed for the capitol on December 28. Two days later the Blossom
dropped her anchor in Monterey Bay where the supplies that had been purchased were taken on board, and a few spars cut. Through the assistance of W. E. P. Hartnell, a naturalized Californian of English birth,
Beechey was able to obtain other supplies from the Mission. However, on
January 6, 1827, the Blossom sailed for the Sandwich Islands in hopes of
obtaining the stores which had not been found in California.

---

37. F. W. Beechey, Narrative of a Voyage to the Pacific and
Beering's (sic) Strait (London, 1831), p. vii.
38. Ibid., p. xii.

Beechey's account of his visit includes extensive observations on the Indians. He also writes briefly about the mission system, the white inhabitants and their customs, and the birds and animals which had been seen. The future of San Francisco Bay is of particular interest to him:

> Situated in the northern hemisphere, between the parallels of
> 22° and 39°, no fault can be found with its climate; its soil
> in general is fertile, it possesses forests of oak and pine
> convenient for building and contributing to the necessities
> of vessels, plains overrun with cattle, excellent ports, and
> navigable rivers to facilitate inland communication.....It is
> evident, from the natural course of events, and from the
> rapidity with which observation has recently been extended
> to the hitherto most obscure parts of the globe that this
> indifference cannot continue, for either it must disappear
> under the present authorities, or the country will fall into
> other hands...[39]

Beechey was impressed, as were most other observers, by the lack of defenses at both Monterey and San Francisco.

After leaving Monterey the _Blossom_ proceeded to the Sandwich Islands, thence to China, and finally back to Bering Strait in the summer of 1827, again in hopes of meeting Franklin or Parry. Again turned back by the approach of winter, Beechey arrived in Monterey, October 29, 1827. The fresh vegetables which were obtained quickly cured the scurvy which had broken out among a portion of his crew. On the 17th of November, the ship was forced to go to San Francisco for fresh water, the supply at Monterey being blackish and contaminated with soap suds.

The _Blossom_ sailed from San Francisco homeward bound on December 3, 1827. It is interesting to note that on Beechey's chart the area, comprising what is now northern California, Oregon, and Washington, is lettered "New Albion," keeping alive the tradition of the English claim to this region.

c. BELCHER

In December, 1835, Beechey was again sent on a scientific-exploratory voyage to the Pacific, this time in the _Sulphur_, which was accompanied by the _Starling_. At Valparaiso, because of sickness, Beechey was forced to relinquish command of the expedition to the next senior officer, Acting Commander Kellett. Kellett was in turn superseded by Captain Sir Edward Belcher, who had been sent out from England for that purpose. The final change of command took place at Panama in February of 1837.[40]

---

39. Beechey, op. cit., p. 393.
40. For an account of this voyage see Captain Sir Edward Belcher, _Narrative of a Voyage Around the World, etc._ (London, 1843).

This expedition had been commissioned to make hydrographic observations in the Atlantic and Pacific Oceans. It was to establish or disprove the existence of several reported islands and reefs, to make observations of weather, currents, magnetic variation, etc., and to conduct a survey of certain parts of the Pacific coast line of South and Central America. Because of anticipated bad weather during a portion of the year, the explorers were instructed to make use of this time in other areas. Their instructions read:

On the approach, therefore, of the monsoon to the coast of Peru, you are to make the utmost expedition in removing both vessels to California, where San Francisco offers a healthy and convenient spot for fresh rating the chronometers. Little is known of this great country except that it is rapidly increasing in population and commerce, and as it contains but few harbours, its shore steep, and the approaches bold, there will be little motive for detention between San Francisco and the district visited by Captain Vancouver.[41]

It seems that natural history was not to be neglected altogether for Belcher was instructed "...to prepare a berth for the botanical collector for plants and seeds for his Majesty's garden at Kew..."[42]

Belcher's expedition finally arrived off San Francisco October 19, 1837, after carrying out its other instructions. Belcher, familiar with San Francisco Bay as a result of his cruise with Beechey ten years earlier, decided to take the Sulphur in that night. She anchored shortly after midnight, and the Starling stood in the following day.

He was not favorably impressed with the changes that had occured since his last visit. "At daybreak I was anxious to take a peep at our old ground, and was much surprised to find everything going to decay, and infinitely worse than we found them ten years before."[43] The secularization of the missions also disappointed him. "The missions, the only respectable establishments in this country, are thus annihilated; they have been virtually plundered by all parties."[44] Belcher continued:

Taking into consideration the whole port of San Francisco, the Sacramento, and minor streams, there is immense field for capital, if the government could protect its citizens or those inclined to reside. At this moment (December 1837) they are reduced to almost their extreme gasp, harassed by their own servants (who are natives) deserting and carrying

41. Belcher, op. cit., p. xviii.
42. Ibid., p. xx.
43. Ibid., p. 116.
44. Belcher, op. cit., pp. 117-118.

off their property; threatened by the Delawares, who have piratically ranged the country, taking away horses and cattle; disturbed by their late <u>declaration</u> and <u>recantation</u> of independence; they sadly want the interposition of some powerful friend to rescue them. To Great Britain their hopes are directed; why, I cannot learn, but I am much inclined to think that it is rather from a pusillanimous fear, and want of energy to stand by each other and expel their common enemies, than from any friendly feeling to Great Britain.[45]

While in San Francisco Bay, Belcher undertook a survey of the Sacramento River. He also searched for the San Joaquin and the Jesus Maria Rivers, which Beechey had reported, but was unable to find them. The Jesus Maria was non-existent, and the San Joaquin was further south than Belcher had anticipated. The Sacramento was charted for a distance of approximately one hundred and fifty miles, an operation which took the party from October 24 to November 18. On this excursion, Belcher described briefly the Indians encountered, as well as the topography of the countryside, and the vegetation, and wild life observed along the river.

Among other trials that the inhabitants were suffering, Belcher reported that they were "...pestered by a set of renegado deserters from whalers and merchant ships."[46] To this group his expedition added "...the serjeant and corporal of marines, carpenter's mate, and several men and boys."[47]

Sailing from San Francisco Bay on November 30, the expedition arrived in Monterey on December 2. "Monterey I found as much increased as San Francisco had fallen into ruin. It was still, however, very miserable, and wanting in the military air of 1827."[48] Belcher was able to obtain a supply of beef, pork, flour, and biscuits. On December 6 the <u>Sulphur</u> sailed for San Blas, the <u>Starling</u> having been dispatched a few days earlier.

In September, 1839, Belcher was again off the coast of California. After dropping down to San Francisco, he sailed to Bodega Bay and made a survey of that area. The expedition then returned to San Francisco to obtain a supply of meat and vegetables. A few days later Belcher continued on down the coast stopping briefly at Monterey, Santa Barbara, San Pedro, San Juan Capistrano, and San Diego, constructing a chart of the coast as he proceeded southward. The <u>Starling</u> was also dispatched to examine Santa Catalina Island and its anchorages.

The <u>Sulphur</u> eventually sailed across the Pacific to Singapore where orders were received to proceed to the China coast. After taking an active part in the Opium War, she reached Spithead, July, 1842.

---

45. <u>Ibid.</u>, p. 134.
46. <u>Ibid.</u>, p. 116.
47. <u>Ibid.</u>, p. 134.
48. Belcher, <u>op</u>. <u>cit</u>., p.136.

5. BRITISH WARSHIPS IN CALIFORNIA

Twice during the period that Spain ruled California, she and England were at war. In 1779 a reluctant Spain was drawn into the American Revolutionary War by France, her fellow member of the "Family Compact." Peaceful relations were reestablished in 1783 by the Treaty of Paris. Thirteen years later, after temporarily aiding the anti-French forces in the period of the French Revolution, on August 19, 1796, Spain signed with France an anti-British pact at San Ildefonson. From that time until 1808, when Joseph Bonaparte was made King of Spain, she sided with France against England and the coalitions which the latter organized.

California was far removed from the theaters of operations, and no hostile acts were committed against her. Spain's participation in the American War lasted, as far as was known in California, from 1780 to 1784. Its only effect in this remote province was a "voluntary" contribution from each Spaniard of two dollars and from each Indian of one dollar to aid the war effort.[49]

In peaceful times, English men-of-war, as well as men-of-war from other nations, stopped in California to obtain fresh supplies, to make repairs, and to offer recreation to their crews. In addition to the warships commanded by Vancouver, Beechey, and Belcher on their exploring expeditions, there is evidence of the following English naval vessels having been in California waters:

    1795 Resolution, Active
    1796 Providence
    1797 Active
    1804 Active
    1814 Issac Todd (armed merchantman), Raccoon
    1818 Blossom
    1841 Curacoa
    1844 Modeste
    1845 America

William Heath Davis, a San Francisco merchant prone to liberal estimations, states that at least one British war vessel would visit California every year. It would generally anchor at Sausalito where Captain Richardson, the British-born harbor master, entertained the crew. He further states that foreigners residing in California thought that these ships had been sent by the British government to observe the province with a view to eventual annexation.[50]

6. CONCLUSION

From the time of Elizabeth's glorious reign, when England was to

---

49. Bancroft, Calif., I, 427-428.
50. William Heath Davis, Seventy-Five Years in California (San Francisco, 1929), p. 154.

embark upon her great colonizing period, California was known to that nation as a remote yet desirable section of the New World. However, England was content to allow her ill-founded claim to that region lapse, and the favorable descriptions of later explorers produced no greater results, as far as political connections with California were concerned.

The reasons for England's failure to act are not hard to find. In the first place her colonizing ventures were conducted as private enterprises, and questions of national expediency, such as the establishment of a colony on the Pacific Coast of North America, were seldom uppermost. Secondly, California was far away. Sending a colonizing expedition to that region would have been incredibly difficult, and healthy commercial relations with such a colony, had it been established, would have been impossible to maintain in the seventeenth century. Thirdly, suitable regions for colonizing were much nearer at hand. When Englishmen looked abroad for new homes, soon after Drake's "Famous Voyage," it was quite naturally to the nearest portion of the New World similar to their Motherland. The Atlantic Coast of North America offered a seemingly unlimited area for commercial exploitation and settlement.

In later years when English colonizing ventures finally extended to the Pacific area, California had been claimed and settled by another nation. English settlements in the Pacific in the nineteenth century were made in regions uninhabited by European peoples and over which only remote foreign claims could be made.

CHAPTER II

CALIFORNIA AND THE FOREIGNERS

1. INTRODUCTION

Although neither Great Britain nor any other European nation was to dispute seriously the Spanish claim to California (excluding Russia's temporary, isolated Bodega-Fort Ross settlement), a trickle of foreign immigration was to invade the province. The Spanish colonial system, which was extended to California in 1769 with the first Spanish settlement, was exclusive -- proscribing not only foreign settlers but foreign traders as well. However, this exclusiveness could not be maintained, especially by a power as weak as nineteenth-century Spain, and inroads were soon made, first on the Spanish commercial monopoly and shortly thereafter on the residential restriction. It must be remembered that this incursion was made by scattered, casual, individual efforts, for personal reasons, and was completely separated from national drives.

All foreigners who came in contact with California in the first decades of Spanish and Mexican rule came by sea. It was not until 1826 that Jedediah Smith and his companions completed the first overland trip from the United States, and many more years were to elapse before the overland approaches from the north and the east were to acquire any significance. The alien ships that touched at California in its pre-United States days can be divided into three classes: scientific and exploratory,[1] men-of-war, and commercial. These ships were to acquaint

---

1. The last half of the eighteenth century and the first half of the nineteenth century witnessed great activity on the part of Europe in the exploration of the rest of the world. This movement had political, scientific, and economic causes. European nations were interested in discovering new lands for purposes of colonization and trade. Exploring expeditions also offered good opportunities to investigate the political, economic, and military strength of the places visited. Another cause was the perennial search for a trade route to the Far East, north of the American continents, and control of that route if found. A purely scientific interest was also involved, and these expeditions were equipped to observe and report on the unknown lands -- their flora, fauna, and human inhabitants.

During the period of its rule by Spain and Mexico, California was visited by scientific-exploratory expeditions from France, Russia, and the United States, in addition to the British voyagers referred to in Chapter I. In general these expeditions were hospitably received and were permitted to carry out their scientific investigations with little hindrance from the provincial authorities. The Californians were glad of the opportunity to entertain well-educated foreigners and to receive news of other parts of the world.

The first of the explorers to reach California after its colonization was the Frenchman, La Perouse. Sailing into Monterey in September,

the outside world with this isolated land, to awaken in other nations interest in it, and to leave upon its shores the forerunners of the non-Spanish pioneers who were to make inevitable its loss by Spain and Spanish America.

Of most significance in the foreign invasion of California are the ships which came primarily for economic purposes. Greater in number than the exploring ships and war vessels, they broke down traditional Spanish barriers against foreign trade and established commercial relations between this province and the rest of the world. They also brought most of the foreigners who came before the eighteen-forties.

2. TRADE UNDER SPANISH RULE

a. SPANISH MONOPOLIZATION OF TRADE

From the time that California was settled it was fitted into the Spanish colonial economic system, which called for Spanish monopolization of all trade and industry. Spain was no exception in wishing to dominate the commercial activity of her colonies. Up through the eighteenth century most European nations subscribed to the mercantilist theory of trade: colonies were held to exist for the benefit of the mother country and trade with them was to be the exclusive privilege of the mother country. "From the discovery of America, trade with the New World, and even the right to reside there, was reserved, except for a very short interval, to subjects of the Spanish Crown. In theory, no foreigners were tolerated."[2]

---

1. Cont'd. from P. 18. - 1785, he was the first foreigner to come in any capacity to the new founded settlement. In 1816 the ship _Rurik_ brought a Russian expedition, commanded by Lieutenant Otto von Kotzebue of the Russian navy, to San Francisco. The expedition was cordially received. /Adelbert von Chamisso, _A Sojourn At San Francisco May 1816_ (San Francisco, 1936), pp. 1-2/ Although von Kotzebue's avowed purpose was to explore the islands of the South Pacific and to search for a northeast passage, it seems probable that he was secretly instructed "...to investigate how much power of resistance there was left in the dying organism of the Spanish colonial empire; or to express it in other terms, to what degree the defiance of Spanish rights could be carried with impunity." /August C. Mahr, _The Visit of the Rurik to San Francisco in 1816_ (Stanford University, 1932), p. 23./ In 1824 von Kotzebue again visited California with a scientific expedition, this time in the ship _Predpriate_. /Bancroft, _op. cit._, 11, 522-523./
   In 1841 an exploring expedition of the United States under the command of Lieutenant Charles Wilkes arrived in San Francisco Bay. On August 7th the _Vincennes_ dropped her anchor, and two months later a second contingent of the expedition, the _Porpoise_, the _Flying Fish_, and the _Oregon_, reached that port./Charles Wilkes, _Narrative of the United States Exploring Expedition during the Years 1838, 1839, 1840, 1841, 1842_ (5 vols., Philadelphia, 1850)./
   2. Clarence Henry Haring, Trade and Navigation Between Spain and the Indies in the Time of the Hapsburgs (Cambridge, 1918), p. 96.

Foreign ships and foreign goods were ruled out of the California trade. However, Spanish laws went even further and forbade trade with Spanish ships, other than the regular transports from San Blas and the Manila galleon, and in Spanish-American goods, other than those brought by these ships.[3] Spanish commercial policy in regard to California was defined by Bucareli, the viceroy of New Spain, in a letter dated August 17, 1773. It was addressed to Rivera y Moncada as he was about to lead a soldier-settler party to California and to relieve Fages as governor. The letter read:

> The admission of foreign boats into the American ports of the king's dominions is absolutely prohibited by the laws of the Indies, and it is commanded in many royal decrees and orders that this prohibition be observed; and there are also repeated decrees that commerce is not to be permitted, even in Spanish ships, on the coasts comprised in this viceroyalty, except in the ships from the Philippines, which comes to Acapulco, and the boats in the ship-yard of San Blas for the support of old and new California.[4]

It became customary for two of the transports to visit California each year. One of them would usually supply San Diego and Santa Barbara, and the other, San Francisco and Monterey.[5] In addition, the Manila galleon was required by law to stop at Monterey on the return trip from Manila to Acapulco. However, the captains of the galleons were anxious to complete their voyages and would often by-pass Monterey, perferring to pay the fine imposed. Even when the galleon did stop, all trade with the ship, except for supplying it with fresh provisions, was prohibited.[6]

The transports each year brought goods which had been ordered by the presidios and missions the preceding year. No other goods were permitted, and precautions were taken to prevent smuggling by the soldiers, sailors, and friars. However, beginning with the year 1785, the individuals living in California could send and receive goods provided there was sufficient room after the official invoices had been filled and provided that no foreign goods were introduced.[7]

Certain abuses soon appeared in this system for the officers and sailors on the transports began to monopolize the nonofficial trade.

---

3. Bancroft, op. cit., I, 624-625; Hubert Howe Bancroft, California Pastoral 1769-1848 (San Francisco, 1888, p. 46. Bancroft's History of California will henceforth be indicated as Calif.
4. Charles Edward Chapman, The Founding of Spanish California: the Northwestward Expansion of New Spain, 1687-1783 (New York, 1916), p. 219.
5. Bancroft, Calif., I, 444.
6. Bancroft, Calif., I, 442.
7. Ibid., I, 624-625.

In April, 1803, the viceroy issued orders prohibiting the ship's company from trading at all, or from refusing to carry the goods of private individuals and traders whenever cargo space permitted.[8] During these early years California exported nothing aside from the supplies furnished to the Manila galleon and an occasional cargo of salt carried by the returning transport.[9]

b. THE SEA OTTER HUNTERS

In spite of official efforts to establish and maintain a Spanish monopoly of California trade, it was not long before ships and traders of various nations were battering down the restrictions which excluded them from this valuable trading opportunity. The first to come were the sea otter hunters.

In the middle of the eighteenth century the Russians began pushing eastward from their Siberian bases in search of the sea otter, whose fur brought high prices in the China market. Rumors of Russian expansion had been instrumental in promoting Spanish colonization of California.

It was Captain Cook's third voyage, however, which stimulated the extension of the sea otter trade to America. On the Northwest Coast, in 1778, his sailors had obtained a few furs from the Indians, which in the following year, were sold for a great profit in Canton. Spanish officials in the Philippines heard of Cook's success from some of his deserters and soon developed plans for entering the sea otter trade. The Russians founded their first permanent settlement in North America at Kodiak in 1783, and in 1784 the published account of Cook's voyage awakened the interest of English and American traders.[10]

The sea otter was found along the coast line and islands of the North Pacific from Yezo in northern Japan, up the coast of Asia, across the Aleutian archipelago, and down the coast of North America to the middle of the peninsula of Lower California. There appeared to be a slight break in the arc between the strait of Juan de Fuca and approximately Trinidad in northern California. In this area few sea otters were taken. The prize which lured the fur hunters to the naturally inhospitable North Pacific and the officially inhospitable California coast has been described as follows:

> The fur of the otter is more beautiful than that of any other marine animal....Its coat consists of an unusually fine, soft, and dense underfur of about three-fourths of an inch in length, and a few longer and slightly coarser overhairs. At the base

---

8. _Ibid._, II, 185
9. _Ibid._, I, 438.
10. Adele Ogden, _The California Sea Otter Trade 1784-1848_ (Berkeley, California, 1941), pp. 1-3.

or roots the fur is a lustrous white or silver color, darkening toward the ends to black in the finest skins and to various shades of brown in the more common pelts.[11]

The skin was at its prime in the third or fourth year. California furs were generally inferior to those of the north, and although some hunters claimed that furs taken in the winter were best, hunting was carried on in California all year long. China was the primary market. In 1790 a skin was worth from $80 to $120. This was abnormally high, however, and in later years the price dropped to one-half or one-third of that amount.

The English were the first to follow up the opportunities which Cook's account portrayed.[12] In 1785 James Hanna sailed to the Northwest Coast from China, and in the next few years several other Englishmen followed his example. Ships commanded by Meares, Tipping, Strange, Lowrie, Guise, Dixon, Portlock, and Hanna were on the Coast in 1786. In 1787 Portlock and Dixon returned, and newcomers Colnett, Duncan, and Barclay put in their appearance. The Americans, who along with the Russians were eventually to dominate the sea otter trade, appeared for the first time in 1788.

News of the sea otter trade in the North Pacific, and publication of the record of Captain Cook's last voyage, stimulated Spain into an attempt to monopolize the trade, as far as California was concerned, for herself. In September, 1784, Vicente Vasadre y Vega presented to the viceroy of New Spain a plan whereby the Spanish government would collect sea otter skins along the California coast. It would then exchange them in China for quicksilver to be used in the mines of Mexico.

The plan was finally approved, and in 1786 Vasadre arrived in California, where, in a short period, he collected 1,060 skins. Proceeding to the Orient, he ran into unexpected difficulties. Opposed by the Philippine Company and government officials in Manila, lacking in trading experience, meeting diplomatic obstacles in Canton, and finding the market glutted by furs from the Northwest Coast, he was forced to conclude an unsatisfactory sale. Although government collection of furs in California continued, there too complications arose, and in 1790 the project was abandoned.[13] In the next few years several other plans for controlling the sea otter trade were proposed, but none of them were put into effect.

The English were the first non-Spanish people to search for sea otters in the waters off California as they also had been further north.[14]

---

11. Ogden, op. cit., p. 4.
12. For an account of the following voyages see Hubert Howe Bancroft, History of the Northwest Coast (San Francisco, 1892), I, 173-190.
13. Bancroft, Calif., I, 438-442.
14. Information on the following English ships is taken from Ogden, op. cit.

Early in 1793 the Butterworth, a ship of 392 tons, commanded by William Brown and owned by Alderman Curtis and others in London, arrived off Santa Cruz. From March 13 to March 15 she was off San Francisco and sailed thence to the Northwest Coast. This ship was again in the waters along the California coast in 1794. In 1793 the Jackal also appeared in California. She was commanded by Alexander Stewart (later William Brown) and was also owned by Alderman Curtis and others in London. Her first recorded stop was at Monterey, and on March 15 she was at Bodega Bay. She then proceeded to the Northwest Coast. The Prince Lee Boo, a sloop of 30-40 tons, commanded by Captain Sharp (later Captain Gordon), and owned by the same company as the Butterworth and the Jackal, also arrived in California in 1793. From January to March, 1793 she was in Bodega Bay. She then sailed to Monterey, back to Bodega Bay, thence to San Francisco, and finally to the northward. The fourth English fur trader to put into California's ports was the Jenny, which arrived in April, 1794. She was a ship of 78 tons, commanded by John William Adamson and owned by Sidenham Teast of Bristol. The fifth and last of the early English sea otter hunters was the bark Phoenix. She was commanded by Hugh Moore, and her owners were located in Bengal. The Phoenix was off Santa Barbara from August 28 to September 5, 1795. From that time until the Northwest Company's brig Columbia picked up a few pelts in 1817, there were no English ships participating in the sea otter trade in California.

Both in California and on the Northwest Coast the English withdrew from this activity.[15] The principal reasons for English withdrawal were: (1) the opposition of the East India Company to the encroachment of the hunters on its trading monopoly in China, where they sold their furs; (2) the Napoleonic Wars which hampered English trade; and (3), as far as California was concerned, the provision of the first Nootka Convention by which England agreed to cease all commercial relations with that province.

Traders of other nations were more successful, and "with the arrival in 1796 of the first Boston vessel, the contest between the otter men and the upholders of the Spanish mercantile system began."[16] Sailing up and down the coast, these ships would barter with the Indians, missionaries,[17]

---

15. From 1785 to 1789 there had been fourteen English ships engaged in the sea otter trade in the north, compared to two American. From 1790 to 1818 there were one hundred and eight American vessels and only twenty-two English, and most of these were before 1800. Bancroft, Northwest Coast, I, 359.

16. Ogden, op. cit., p. 32.

17. Under the Vasadre plan the missions were the primary collection points for the skins because they controlled the Indians. When that plan failed, the missions continued to gather skins, which they now sold to foreigners. In 1806 Guardian Jose Gasol issued a series of regulations for the guidance of the California friars. It read in part, "in order

and soldiers, exchanging goods for otter skins. Every effort was made by the Spanish officials to prevent such trade, but their counter-measures were usually ineffective. In 1803, however, brazen defiance of governmental authority prompted drastic means of controlling the contra-bandistas.[18] In that year "the battle of San Diego" had been fought when the _Lelia Byrd_ was caught smuggling in San Diego Bay. Her captain, Richard Cleveland, decided to make a run for it and succeeded in reaching the open sea after carrying on an artillery duel with the shore battery.[19]

So successful were the new regulations that the traders were forced to change their strategy. Agreements were made between American ship owners and the Russian American Fur Company. The latter, at its settle-ments in Alaska, would furnish groups of Aleut hunters and their baidarkas (kayaks) to the American ships.[20] Sailing to the California coast, the trading ships would then act as tenders for the Aleuts as they put off in their baidarkas to hunt the sea otters. The furs thus accumulated were divided equally between the ship owner and the Russian American Fur Company. The officials of California were helpless against this system as they had no ships with which to drive off the poachers.

The Russians were not content to share the trade with others, how-ever, and in 1809 they began completely independent operations, although

---

17. Cont'd from P. 23. - to avert the reprimand which the college would have to suffer from the viceroy if it should come to his knowledge that any of your reverences was trading with the foreigners, I expressly order that no one either directly or indirectly trade with them." Cited in Bancroft, _Calif._, II, 42. It was not so much the sin of smuggling as it was the sin of being caught. The traders agreed that the mission-aries were excellent customers. _Ibid._ Basol's instructions were not complied with. When the _Mercury_ was captured for smuggling in 1813, Captain Eayrs produced letters from various padres which indicated that trade with them was being carried on at that time. Irving Berdine Richman, _California Under Spain and Mexico 1535-1847_ (Boston and New York, 1911), p. 204.
18. An order from the Viceroy to the Governor of California dated Jan. 12, 1805, closed all ports in the Spanish dominions to all but national mail vessels. Bancroft, _Calif._, II, 31. When Arrillaga became governor in 1806, he stated that, although as a rule the smuggl-ing ships could not be captured, this was to be done if possible. His solution was to prevent the people from trading with the foreigners, thus removing the reason for their being on the coast. On the arrival of a vessel the nearest presidio was to be notified, no supplies were to be given, and a strict guard was to be set up on the shore. No citizen was to leave his home while the vessel remained, and suspicious people were to be arrested. _Ibid._, II, 35-36.
19. H.W.S. Cleveland, _Voyages of a Merchant Navigator of the Days that are Past_ (New York, 1886), pp. 94-95.
20. Bancroft, _Calif._, II, 83-96.

a few contracts with American ships were continued until 1812. Non-Russian ships had again, therefore, to resort to illicit trade with the Californians. Conditions for such maneuvers were more propitious at this time because the Mexican independence movement prevented the San Blas transports from making their annual voyages. Being cut off from their normal source of manufactured goods, the inhabitants were anxious for the opportunity to trade with the foreigners. On the other hand, the Spanish officials were more successful in their counter-measures in the next few years, and captured the _Mercury_,[21] the _Pedler_, and the _Lydia_. However, the _Pedler_ and the _Lydia_ were both freed within a few days for lack of evidence.[22]

When California passed from Spanish to Mexican rule in 1822, trade with foreign vessels was legalized. It was now possible to barter for or buy sea otter furs from the residents of California without resorting to subterfuges. However, the numbers of furs obtained rapidly declined as the sea otter approached extinction, and under Mexican rule efforts were made to restrict the hunting of these animals to Mexican citizens by a system of licensing. It was the naturalized citizens, though, that received most benefit from this restriction, as the American-born hunters soon adapted themselves to hunting on the sea.[23] Steps were also taken to regulate a new group of unlicensed foreign ships operating off the coast. By the time of the American conquest the sea otter trade had dwindled to relative insignificance.

c. THE WHALING SHIPS

The second group of foreign commercial ships to come to California and to encroach upon the Spanish were the whaling ships of all nations which cruised the Pacific. As these ships were frequently absent from their home ports for two or three years, it was necessary for them to put in to friendly ports for fuel, water, and fresh supplies, to make repairs, and to offer liberty and recreation to their crews. The greatest number of whalers usually arrived in California in the early fall.[24]

Although Spanish laws prohibited commercial intercourse with foreign vessels, at no time were ships in need of repairs or supplies turned away. Under the Spanish regime whalers were permitted to buy fresh vegetables and meat for the ship's own consumption. The supplies most commonly purchased were bullocks, sheep, lambs, potatoes, beans, pumpkins, onions, and apples.[25] Not infrequently the sailors had to go

21. Richman, _op. cit._, pp. 203-205.
22. Bancroft, _Calif._, II, 2-3, 213.
23. Nicholas Dawson, _California in '41; Texas in '51_ (San Francisco, 1933), pp. 37-51.
24. Duflot de Mofras, _Duflot de Mofras' Travels on the Pacific Coast_ (2 vols., Santa Ana, Calif., 1937), I, 210.
25. Adele Ogden, "Havens for Whalers," _The Grizzly Bear_, January, 1936, p. 3.

ashore to gather the vegetables and to butcher the cattle themselves.[26]

Whaling ships were known to have visited Monterey,[27] Santa Barbara, Yerba Buena, San Diego, and other ports.[28] But Sausalito, on the northern side of San Francisco Bay, became their favorite anchorage.[29] It was sometimes known as Whalers' Bay or Whalers' Harbor.[30] Sausalito was chosen because of its easily accessible and plentiful supply of fresh water.[31] No other port in California offered this advantage.[32] Sausalito was also desirable because of its deep water, nearby wood supply, and the fact that it was far enough removed from the revenue agent in Yerba Buena to permit illegal trade.

When trade had become legalized under Mexican rule, it became customary for these ships to carry a small stock of goods to barter for the supplies needed. Mexican law allowed each whaling vessel to trade up to $400 worth of goods duty free, but they were not permitted to sell goods for for cash because this would circumvent Mexican import duties. Such trade was highly beneficial to the Californians, who were in constant need of manufactured articles, and this merchandise, coming in duty free, was much lower in price than that passing through the regular channels. Moreover, these goods could be paid for in agricultural produce rather than in money, which was always scarce in California. The Californians were anxious to grow the types of vegetables that the whalers wanted in order to be able to barter with them.[33]

Being subject to little supervision, the whalers frequently did not adhere to the $400 limit placed on their trade, and they were able to conduct a flourishing business without interference from the Mexican officials.[34]

In spite of the benefits that trade with the whaling ships brought

---

26. Ogden, "Havens," loc. cit., p. 3.
27. Mofras, op. cit., P. 211.
28. Davis, op. cit., p. 154.
29. Ogden, Havens" loc. cit., p. 3.
30. Sir George Simpson, Narrative of a Journey Round the World, During the Years 1841 and 1842 (2 vols., London, 1847), I, 282; Mofras, op. cit., I, 233.
31. Davis, op. cit., p. 154.
32. Mofras, op. cit., I, 210. Monterey's water supply was notoriously inconvenient. Before 1844 whalers often had to dig their own wells. In that year Larkin, the American consul, constructed a permanent well for them. Ogden, "Havens," loc. cit.
33. Davis, op. cit., p. 155.
34. William Heath Davis relates how he and other merchants in Yerba Buena would visit the whaling ships in the bay at night. They would buy up the ships' excess stock, and since no duty had been paid, they could sell it for a great profit. Davis, op. cit., p. 156.

to California, an illiberal economic policy tended to stifle it. In 1833 it was reported in the Departmental State Papers that the heavy tonnage duty was driving away whalers to the Sandwich Islands. A tonnage duty of one real per ton was recommended[35] instead of the seventeen reals per ton then being charged.[36] This fee was paid only once for each visit to the coast and so it was not excessive for trading ships which might touch at each of several ports many times.[37] However, for whalers which usually anchored only once, it was an exorbitant duty. In 1841 Sir George Simpson, Governor General of the Hudson's Bay Company, when visiting California, reported that although whalers used to refit in that province, they were going to the Sandwich Islands instead. The reasons given were that the Islands offered a better supply of competent labor, both native and foreign, and that the customs duties were more reasonable.[38]

The number of whalers that annually entered the ports of California is difficult to determine because few records of their arrival were kept. They avoided Monterey to escape the payment of tonnage duties, and, in other ports, anchored far from the customs house so that their illicit trading activities would not be interrupted. The whaling ships stayed in port for only a brief time and had little intercourse with the merchants, whose records serve as a source of information for other types of ships.[39] William Heath Davis, one of the early pioneers, stated that

----

35. Departmental State Papers, Benicia Customs House, II, 8. Cited in Bancroft, Calif., III, 369.

36. W.S.W. Ruschenberger, Narrative of a Voyage Round the World During the Years 1835, 36, and 37 (London, 1838), II, 405. Seventeen reals would be $2.12½. Bancroft states that the rate was $2.50 per ton. Bancroft, Calif., III, 117. In 1836 the tonnage rate was reduced to eight reals per ton. Ibid., III, 476.

37. Captain Phelps of the Alert stated that on its cruise of 1840-1843, his ship stopped at San Francisco 7 times, Monterey 13 times, Santa Cruz 3 times, St. Louis /?/ 4 times, Santa Barbara 17 times, Refugio 5 times, and "the depot", (probably San Diego) 10 times. In all the bower anchor was dropped 131 times. William D. Phelps, Fore and Aft; or Leaves from the Life of an Old Sailor (Boston, 1871), p. 268.

38. Simpson, op. cit., I, 28-289. In the year from Sept., 1840, to Sept., 1841, 53 English and American whalers stopped at the Sandwich Islands, while only 12 put in to California's ports, according to Mofras, op. cit., I, 267-268.

39. Whatever the total number might have been, the proportion of British whalers was much less than that of American ships. The following British whalers are mentioned in Bancroft's list of ships, which is admittedly incomplete: Discovery, 1820; Orion, 1822; Favorite, 1827; Isabella, 1827; Recovery, 1825; Times, 1828; Brixon, 1836; Indian, 1837; and Toward Castle, 1837.

there would be thirty or forty whalers in San Francisco Bay at one time.[40] Presumably, this would be for only a short time in the fall when nearly all of the whalers sought some port. Other observers give more conservative figures.[41]

Desertions from whalers were common, and they were responsible for leaving in California many of the non-Spanish pioneers.[42]

d. FIRST AUTHORIZED FOREIGN TRADE.

Although sea otter traders and whaling ships offered an opportunity for trade on a small scale under the Spanish regime, commercial relations with foreigners were still legally prohibited. The first break in the official attitude came in 1806 when Governor Arrillaga authorized the Russian, Nicholas Petrovich Rezanof, to barter approximately $7,000 worth of goods for grain.[43]

In 1805 Rezanof, the Chamberlain of the Czar, visited the Russian-American Fur Company outpost of Sitka on a tour of inspection. He found that colony on the verge of collapse because of scurvy caused by improper food, and in danger of actual starvation. Although knowing that trade with California was prohibited, he decided that breaking down the restrictions offered the only hope of relief for the Alaskan outpost. As a result he purchased the American ship _Juno_ and sailed for California with a cargo of goods which he hoped to exchange for food.[44] When the Russians reached San Francisco Bay, they were cordially received by the inhabitants. After social obligations had been duly performed, Rezanof began diplomatic negotiations with Don Jose Arguello, commandant of the presidio, and Don Jose Arrillaga, the governor. It was a very delicate situation for he realized that the desperate need of the Alaskan colony must not become known to the Spanish officials. If they were aware of the actual situation at Sitka, the Spaniards would surely enforce the trade restrictions, thus forcing the Russians to withdraw from North America. All of Rezanof's diplomatic skill was in vain, for Arrillaga insisted upon rigid compliance with the law forbidding trade, and rumors of war between Russia and France and her allies made the situation even more difficult. However, Rezanof was not yet defeated. His solution to this impasse resulted in one of California's most famous love stories.

---

40. Davis, _op. cit._, p. 154.
41. See Bancroft's annual list of ships.
42. Mofras states that American and English whalers were troubled with desertion. In 1839 the French ship _Joseph_ had 14 deserters out of a crew of 25. Mofras, _op. cit._, 1, 263.
43. For an account of this episode see Bancroft, _Calif._, II, 264-277.
44. Nicholas Petrovich Rezanov, _The Rezanov Voyage to Nueva California in 1806_ (San Francisco, 1926), p. 5.

It so happened that Don Jose Arguello had a very lovely young daughter, Dona Concepcion, whom Rezanof described as "the universally recognized beauty of Nueva California." After a brief courtship, Rezanof succeeded in winning her heart, and the two became engaged to be married. As the prospective son-in-law of Don Jose, Rezanof's bargaining position was enhanced considerably, and Arrillaga authorized the transaction which the Russians desired.[45]

Because of this voyage, Fort Ross was established in 1812 by the Russians as a permanent source of California grain, as well as the headquarters for her sea otter hunters on the California coast.[46]

Although Spanish rule continued in California until 1822, and this province was always loyal to the mother country, revolutionary events in Mexico and other parts of Latin America weakened the authority of Spanish commercial restrictions. In 1811 the San Blas transports were discontinued,[47] and California thus lost her only legal means of supply. Partial relief was furnished by a few Spanish ships from Lima, but it eventually became necessary for the governors to permit a limited amount of trade with foreign ships.

The second official authorization of trade occured in 1816 when Governor Sola allowed the Northwest Company's brig Colonel to barter goods for flour and other produce, to the extent of $6,796.[48] From that time to the end of his administration, Sola was forced to let down the bars on foreign trade because of the great need for manufactured goods.[49] There was little need to resort to smuggling for the provincial authorities were glad to purchase cargoes that could be paid for in mission

---

45. It was arranged that the marriage would take place after Rezanof completed a proposed trip to Moscow and Madrid, but he died in Siberia before he could return to claim his bride. Some doubt has been cast upon Rezanof's motives by the statement of his companion, Georg von Langsdorff. The latter wrote, "The bright eyes of Dona Concepcion had made a deep impression upon his heart; and he conceived that a nuptial union with the daughter of the Commandant at St. Francisco would be a vast step gained towards promoting the political objects he had so much at heart. He had therefore nearly come to a resolution to sacrifice himself by this marriage to the welfare, as he hoped, of the two countries /Spain and Russia/." /Georg von Langsdorff, Voyages and Travels in Various Parts of the World During the Years 1803, 1804, 1805, 1806, 1807, II, 183. Cited in Bancroft, Calif., II, 72./ There can be little doubt of Dona Concepcion's love, however. She refused all other suitors and devoted herself to aiding the poor and the sick.
46. Bancroft, Calif., II, 199-203.
47. Ibid., II, 211.
48. Bancroft, Calif., II, 278.
49. Ibid., II, 216, 251-252, 257, 419.

produce or drafts on the treasury. Making the best of a bad situation, Sola devised a tariff schedule to cover the imports which he had authorized. In August, 1817, he decreed that imports pay the same rates that they had paid as exports at the port of embarkation. In November of that year import and export duties were established on a percentage basis.[50]

3. TRADE UNDER MEXICAN RULE

Mexican independence was finally achieved, after many years of revolution, in 1821. Although California had taken no part in the struggle, she willingly cast in her lot with the new government. One of the first acts of the Mexican government, and one of great significance for California, was the removal of the restrictions on foreign trade. By decree of the Cortes of December 15, 1821, Monterey and San Diego were opened to foreign trade. The following duties were established: 25% on imports, 12% on exports, 6% to be paid by the seller and 6% by the buyer, and a duty of 3.5% on coin exported.[51]

a. THE HIDE AND TALLOW TRADE

As a result of the legalization of trade, the third, and most important, phase of early California commercial activity began. This was the hide and tallow trade. California did not develop as an agricultural community, at this time, because there was no market for this type of export. The commodities which she could produce, and for which she could find a market, were hides and tallow. Consequently, California became a grazing country.[52] The hides were bought by the leather industries of England and New England, and the tallow found a ready market in South America.[53] From these exports the goods which were so greatly desired could be obtained.

This trade had started in a small way under Spanish rule when an occasional cargo of tallow, at $2.50 per arroba, was exported in the San Blas transports on their return trips to Mexico.[54] Beginning in 1813, several Spanish ships from Lima arrived in California to barter cloth

---

50. *Ibid.*, II, 419.
51. Bancroft, *Calif.*, II, 473, 475.
52. The California cattle, described by Bryant and Mofras as large and strong, roamed wild over the countryside and became a menace to people on foot.
53. The Americans sought only hides. Where tallow had been accepted, it was often exchanged for hides with vessels bound for South America. Theodore Gray, "Hide and Tallow in Alta California, under Spanish and Mexican Rule, to 1845 Inclusive, "*The Grizzly Bear*, July, 1917, p. 5.
54. Gray, "Hide and Tallow," *loc. cit.*, p. 5.

and miscellaneous goods for hides and tallow.[55] However, it was not until
1822 that the trade was established on a permanent basis. In that year
W. E. P. Hartnell and Hugh McCulloch, representatives of the English firm
of John Begg & Company, signed a three year contract with the mission
fathers for the products of their herds.[56] It was in that same year that
the American ship Sachem appeared on the coast to begin the American phase
of this commerce.

As finally established the hide and tallow trade became a well organized industry. Trading ships came to California laden with goods which
the inhabitants needed. After clearing their cargoes with the customs
officials in Monterey, the ships sailed along the coast, trading with the
mission fathers and the rancheros.[57] In the first half of the Mexican
period the missions carried on much of the commerce,[58] but after their
secularization, the missions' share sank to relative insignificance. It
is difficult to determine the actual extent of the hide and tallow trade.
William Heath David estimated that from 1826 to 1848, 1,250,000 hides,
and arrobas of tallow equal to twice that number, were exported.[59]
Mofras, a usually reliable observer, stated that in the year 1838, 200,000
hides were shipped out, but that the number had fallen to 100,000 in
1841.[60] Lieutenant Wilkes in 1842 observed that the average exports had
been 150,000 hides and 200,000 arrobas of tallow.[61]

The ships which came to buy hides and tallow offered a great variety
of goods for exchange.[62] In order to display its wares, each ship fitted
up a compartment as a showroom, and samples of the merchandise carried
were stacked on shelves or set forth in show cases.[63] In some instances
temporary warehouses were established on shore at strategic ports, and a
portion of the cargo would be landed for barter while the ship sailed away
to other parts of the province. When the ship returned, the hides taken
in and the unsold merchandise would be put aboard. The arrival of a ship
in port was an exciting event for the inhabitants, all of whom would be
eager to visit her and inspect the stock of goods. The ship's boats at
such times would be kept busy ferrying the natives between the ship and
the shore.

---

55. Gray, "Hide and Tallow," loc. cit., p. 5.
56. Bancroft, Calif., II, 476. See Appendix I for a list of British
trading ships in California.
57. Davis, op. cit., p. 204.
58. In 1833 the Volunteer sold $15,000 to $20,000 worth of goods to
Padre Quijas of the Mission Dolores, Ibid., p. 7.
59. Davis, op. cit., pp. 255-257. Specific ships and their cargoes
are listed to account for 1,068,000 hides.
60. Mofras, op. cit., I, 255. In 1834 the missions owned 424,000
head of cattle. Ibid., I, 164. They slaughtered one-third of the herd each
year. Ibid., I, 261.
61. Wilkes, op. cit., V, 158.
62. Dana lists spirits, tea, coffee, sugar, spices, raisins, molasses,
hardware, crockery-ware, tin-ware, cutlery, clothing of all kinds, boots and
shoes, calicos, cottons, furniture, in fact "everything from Chinese fire-
works to English cartwheels." Richard Henry Dana, Jr., Two Years Before the
Mast (Cambridge, Mass., 1911), pp. 93-94.
63. Ibid.

Trade was carried on for cash, for credit, or on a barter basis. An arroba of tallow was worth from $1.50 to $3.00.[64] The value of a hide became fixed at $1.50 in cash or $2.00 in merchandise.[65] Not only did the Californian have to sell low, but he had to buy high.[66] For his $2.00 hide he received an article worth $.75 in Boston,[67] or half a crown or two shillings in London.[68] The missions and wealthy _rancheros_ frequently would bring their hides to the shore and exchange them directly for the goods desired.[69] However, credit was common, and the Californians had a strong sense of honor. It was easy for the _ranchero_ to arrange to pay for his purchases at the next slaughtering season.

In charge of a ship's financial transactions was the supercargo, who acted as its business agent. Traveling overland, ahead of the ship, he notified each community when to expect it and what type of goods it carried. He would take orders and have the goods unloaded from the ship. He would also arrange with his company's creditors for the delivery of their products.[70] Some of the supercargoes became permanent residents of California and established retail stores in the principal communities.

As the California coast line offers no fully protected anchorages aside from San Francisco and San Diego Bays, it was often necessary for the boats to contend with a heavy surf at intermediate points. Passengers were frequently drenched when landing or embarking; but of greater moment was the difficulty which was added to lightering, freight to and from the ships. Even in a moderate surf, loading the boat with hides and then retracting from the beach was a maneuver requiring considerable skill.[71]

During its stay on the coast (usually a period of two or three years)[72] each ship, at regular intervals, would deposit the hides, which it had collected, at San Diego. There they would be treated and stored for eventual reshipment when a sufficient number of hides to fill the vessel had been accumulated. Each ship had its own storehouse on the beach, and a few men were put ashore to carry on the curing process while the ship proceeded northward in quest of more hides.[73] The final loading in San Diego

---

64. Gray, "Hide and Tallow," loc. cit., p. 5.
65. Frank Soule, The Annals of San Francisco (New York, 1855), p. 164.
66. Edwin Bryant, What I Saw in California (Santa Ana, California, 1936), pp. 303-304.
67. Dana, op. cit., p. 94.
68. Simpson, op. cit., I, 289.
69. Alfred Robinson, Life in California, Being a Resident of Several Years in that Territory (San Francisco, 1897), p. 51.
70. Davis, op. cit., pp. 58-60.
71. Dana, op. cit., pp. 72-73.
72. Phelps, op. cit., p. 261, 268.
73. Each man could handle 25 hides per day. Dana, op. cit., p. 187.

was a happy time for the crew for it meant that soon they would be homeward bound.[74]

b. MEXICAN RESTRICTIONS ON TRADE

When California had been officially opened to trade in 1822, it was
only to legalize the commerce which Sola had been forced to permit in
the last years of his administration. For the first years of Mexican
rule there were few restrictive laws on trade, and those that were on
the books were laxly enforced. Gradually a series of regulations were
adopted which tended to confine closely trade along the coast. Before
the restrictive laws are enumerated it is well to realize that in practice they were tempered by smuggling, half-hearted enforcement, and the
custom of granting special permission to disregard the rules.

The most vital restriction on trade was the high import duty. From
the 25% established in 1821, it was increased to $42\frac{1}{2}$% in 1826.[75] In
later years it was further increased to approximately 100%.[76] Import
duties became the primary source of revenue for the provincial government.
In spite of that fact, since both the natives and the merchants were
eager to trade, they collaborated on means of circumventing this restriction.

In 1825 the first of a series of orders limiting trade to specific
ports was issued. Echeandia decreed that all trade was forbidden except
at the four presidial ports: San Diego, Santa Barbara, Monterey, and
San Francisco.[77] In 1826 Herrara, the Mexican government's fiscal agent
in California, following orders from his superior, announced that no
vessel was to load or unload at any other port than Monterey. Echeandia
countermanded the order, provisionally, and it did not go into effect.
His action was approved by the disputacion and the central government.
Two years later, however, the governor decreed that only Monterey was to
be open to foreign traders and that the coasting trade was to be confined
to Mexican ships.[78] The dual purpose of this decree was to stimulate
Mexican commerce and to prevent smuggling by collecting all the duties at
a central point. It had little effect as the natives showed scant interest in commercial activity, and it was never strictly enforced.[79] Traders
were given special licenses or were permitted to trade freely by paying
the expense of a customs guard, who remained on board during the cruise.[80]

When a ship reached Monterey an agreement on duties would be reached,
based on statements, examinations of papers, inspections, and appraisals

---

74. Ibid., p. 327. To load the Alert, which held 40,000 hides, six
weeks of solid work were required.
75. Bancroft, Calif., III, 117.
76. Simpson, op. cit., I, 289; Phelps, op. cit., p. 250.
77. Bancroft, Calif., III, 29.
78. Ibid., III, 117-131.
79. Robinson, op. cit., p. 29.
80. Bancroft, Calif., III, 136.

of cargo.[81] The merchants, of course, tried to make this agreement as favorable as possible. Once it had been reached and the customs duties paid, in whole or in part, the ship was free to sail up and down the coast as a movable showroom.[82]

c. EVASIONS OF TRADE RESTRICTIONS

The strict regulations on trade, established by the Mexican government, were frequently evaded. Foreign traders became proficient in breaking the law. Smugglers remained in good standing in the community, just as did some American smugglers in the revolutionary period of the United States. They rationalized their activities by claiming to sell goods cheaper than the goods could otherwise be sold. William Heath Davis states that the traders were honorable and high-minded men, and had they been required to take an oath, the law would have been respected.[83]

The simplest form of smuggling was to trade without making any pretense of obeying the law. The techniques and practices of the sea otter hunters were quickly adapted to the hide and tallow trade. This form of evasion simply involved trading along the coast without stopping at Monterey to pay duties on the goods exchanged. Smuggling was made easy by the sparse settlement of the coastal area. Ranchos and missions were widely separated, and trading could be carried on with one of them with little probability of unwelcome observation. Government officials were scarce, being located in only the larger settlements.

A second means of smuggling was slightly less crude. Before proceeding to Monterey to pay duties on their cargoes, some traders would land part of it in a secluded spot along the coast.[84] The Santa Barbara Islands became very popular for this purpose.[85] These ships then sailed into Monterey, paid duties only on the goods remaining on board, and obtained the required trading permits. They could then pick up the hidden goods and conduct their businesses under the permits with little to fear from the revenue agents.

A similar practice involved transfer of goods between ships. A vessel which had obtained a license would rendezvous in a hidden cove with one which had not paid duties. Goods would then be transferred from the unlicensed to the licensed ship. The latter would then continue trading with a replenished stock of goods on which no duties were paid.[86] Dana, in Two Years Before the Mast, relates the following

---

81. Ibid., III, 368.
82. Customs duties were paid partly in goods and partly in currency. Mofras states that usually two-thirds were paid in goods. Mofras, op. cit., I, 260.
83. Davis, op. cit., pp. 107-108.
84. Davis, op. cit., pp. 105-106.
85. Ibid., p. 109.
86. Mofras, op. cit., I, 260.

incident:

> The second day after our arrival, a full-rigged brig came
> round the point from the northward, sailed leisurely
> through the bay /Santa Barbara/, and stood off again for
> the southeast in the direction of the large island of
> Catalina. The next day the Avon got under way, and stood
> in the same direction, bound for San Pedro. This might
> do for marines and Californians, but we knew the ropes
> too well. The brig was never seen again on the coast,
> and the Avon went into San Pedro in about a week with a
> replenished cargo of Canton and American goods.[87]

As the Mexican officials in Monterey were seldom diligent in their
inspections, false invoices could be used to good advantage. On these
rigged papers the value of the cargo would be shown to be much less than
it really was. As a result tariffs based on the lowered figures were
proportionally less.[88] Another type of smuggling required the use of
false bottoms or false bulkheads. Goods were hidden in this way, or in
out of the way compartments, so that the Mexican officials overlooked
them in their rather superficial inspection. Davis says: "They
/Mexican officials/ were so exceedingly well mannered that they did not
wish to appear impolite, and so they did not make any critical and
offensive scrutiny of the arrangements and contents of the vessel."[89]

Foreign traders were able to engage in smuggling because of the
laxity of the revenue agents. If they were well treated with food, wine
and gifts, the revenue agents were inclined to be lenient in their
findings. When the officials boarded a ship to determine the customs
duty, they were royally entertained at tables laden with good food, good
wine, and fine cigars. After a cursory inspection, an amicable agreement could be reached.[90]

Besides being lax, Mexican officials were not incorruptible.
Foreign vessels which entered any port before passing through customs
at the provincial capital were required to have a guard placed on board,
who remained there as long as the ship was in port. Once the guard was
on board, he could often be bribed to stay in his cabin while the ship
carried on its smuggling activities.[91] Sometimes the guard was chosen
with this plan in mind. Masters were guided in their choice of ports by
the influence which they had with the local authorities.[92] Subordinate
officials were frequently under the control of the traders.[93]

---

87. Dana, op. cit., p. 260.
88. Davis, op. cit., pp. 107-108.
89. Ibid., pp. 108-109.
90. Davis, op. cit., pp. 262-263.
91. Ibid., pp. 105-106; Bancroft, Calif., IV, 374-375.
92. Bancroft, Calif., IV, 374-375.
93. Ibid., II, 670.

Granting the corruption and laxity of the officials, the fact remains that even had they tried to prevent smuggling, law enforcement agencies were lacking. Revenue agents were few and far between. There was no customs detective force, and, even more important, there were no revenue cutters. For this reason sea otter hunters had been able to sail up and down the coast unopposed. As long as they didn't land on the mainland or come within range of the coastal batteries, they usually had been safe. For this reason smugglers could use the coastal islands and out-of-the-way coves for their unlawful activities. Occasionally, under Spanish rule, one of the transports or one of the Lima ships, when in California waters, would capture a ship suspected of smuggling.[94] For a brief period naval aid was given when the _Princess_ in 1806 and 1807 and the _San Carlos_ in 1808 were on the coast for the specific purpose of discouraging the contrabandistas.[95] But these sporadic efforts could not be effective. In 1823 California acquired a vessel of its own when the Rover was purchased from Captain John Cooper for $9,000,[96] and in 1837 the _California_[97] was purchased from Henry Paty, also for $9,000.[98] However, both of these vessels were used for commercial purposes and had no deterrent effect on the law breakers.

There was still another reason that the laws were not strictly enforced. The foreign traders were in a strong bargaining position because, during the Mexican period, customs duties provided the greater part of the provincial revenue.[99] As a result, the officials in Monterey could not be too strict in their interpretation of the law, for fear of losing what duties the ships would pay.[100] When a vessel arrived with a cargo, threats to take it elsewhere were usually effective in gaining the concessions that the captain desired.[101]

By 1836 the commercial interests in California had become strong enough to influence trading regulations. Soon after assuming the governorship, Alvarado reduced the tonnage duty from seventeen reals to eight reals per ton, authorized foreigners to engage in the coasting trade under a permit from the government, and fixed the import duty at forty percent.[102] This action was presumably taken in recognition of the aid given Alvarado's party by the foreigners.[103] The strength of the commercial interests was again demonstrated in 1843 when the Mexican government issued a decree prohibiting retail trade by foreigners throughout

_____

94. Bancroft, _Calif._, II, 203; Richman, op. cit., pp. 203-205.
95. Bancroft, _Calif._, II, 37, 83.
96. _Ibid._, II, 493.
97. She was an unarmed schooner of 86 tons, carrying a crew of ten. Mofras, op. cit., I, 68.
98. Bancroft, _Calif._, IV, 101.
99. Simpson, op. cit., 1, 359; Mofras, op. cit., I, 168, 263.
100. Mofras, op. cit., I, 168, 263.
101. Bancroft, _Calif._, IV, 206-207.
102. Bancroft, _Calif._, III, 475-476; IV, 83. Later observers state that the tariff usually approximately equalled 100%.
103. _Ibid._, III, 475-476; IV, 83.

the republic. Not only was the decree disregarded in California, but the re-importation of foreign goods from Mexican ports was temporarily prohibited unless full import duties were paid. In addition, an attempt was made to clamp down on the extensive trade being conducted by the whalers. Both of these measures would tend to reduce the competition that the resident foreign merchants were experiencing.[104]

By 1846 the hide and tallow trade was a vital part of California's economy. It supplied her most pressing needs for outside goods, it provided a large part of the province's revenue, and it fixed grazing upon the land as the foremost industry. The hide and tallow trade also brought many foreigners to California. Other foreigners were left by ships hunting the sea otter and by whalers. Exploring expeditions and men-of-war were accountable for still more.[105] It was from the sea that the early pioneers came, and by the time that the overland invasion began, restrictions against foreigners had been broken down, a foreign colony had been established, and in most cases the outsiders were hospitably received.

4. RECEPTION OF FOREIGN RESIDENTS

a. REGULATION OF IMMIGRATION

Foreigners were not welcome in California for many years after its colonization. Just as trade with Spanish colonies was restricted to Spanish subjects, the right of residence was similarly restricted. The Spanish empire was, in theory, a closed corporation. Foreigners were prohibited in order to ensure a homogeneous citizenry, loyal to the mother country. In this way the internal safety of the colony would be assured. In the first decades of Spanish rule in California, despite regulations to the contrary, occasional foreigners, other than welcome guests, did enter the province. These people were left as deserters or because of sickness, by the ships which operated along the coast. At first the deserters were rounded up by the provincial authorities and delivered to their ships or to ships of the same nationality. In other cases they were sent to New Spain for further disposition. Those who were left because of sickness were treated in the same manner as soon as they had recovered.

---

104. _Ibid._, IV, 428-429. In the following year Governor Pico voided the decree requiring repayment of duties and the restrictions on whalers. _Ibid._, IV, 555.
105. It might also be mentioned that the only hostile external force ever directed against California, before the Americans came, was responsible for doubling the number of foreign residents of that time. The de Bouchard expedition of 1818 left four men; Joseph Chapman, John Rose, and two negroes, named Pascual and Norris. Bancroft, _Calif._, II, 202, 248. The orther foreigners in California at that time also numbered four.

In 1796 Governor Borica was presented with an immigration problem of unprecedented magnitude. Captain Ebenezer Dorr in the Otter arrived in Monterey enroute from the Northwest Coast to China with a cargo of furs. He needed water, fresh meat, and other supplies, all of which were furnished without hesitation. On his departure from the capital, Dorr, "forgetting the hospitality he was given,"[106] as Borica expressed it, put ten undesirable men and one woman ashore. While awaiting instructions from the viceroy as to what was to be done with these people, Borica put them all to work. According to Bancroft, "They proved so industrious and well behaved that Borica would fain have retained them in the country, but in obedience to royal orders he was obliged to send them the next year to San Blas enroute for Cadiz."[107] This episode illustrates the Spanish method of dealing with foreigners. Perhaps it explains even better why the prohibition against them was eventually disregarded.

The first foreigner to be permitted to remain in California entered the province in 1814. The English armed merchantman, Issac Todd, came to Monterey, ostensibly bound for Manila, for tea. In reality, she was carrying supplies to the Northwest Fur Company's post on the Columbia River, with the aid of which the American post, Fort Astoria, was to be captured.[108] Three men were left in Monterey by the Issac Todd to recover from scurvy, and eight others deserted. One of the three sick men was John Gilroy, who can claim the distinction of being the first permanent foreign resident in California. What happened to the other ten men is not clear, but it is probable that the deserters were given up to the English man-of-war, Raccoon, which arrived in California later in the year.[109] Why Gilroy was allowed to remain is uncertain, but in 1819, together with John Mulligan and Thomas Doak, he was granted written permission to settle and marry in California.[110]

The leniency shown Gilroy did not establish a precedent, and there was not an immediate influx of foreigners. Most newcomers were shipped off as they had been in the past, and by 1820 there were only thirteen foreign residents in California.[111] Gradually, however, the number of outsiders increased, until in 1830, their number totalled about one hundred and fifty.[112] More lenient restrictions on immigration under Mexican rule and the legalization of trade were responsible for the increase. The hide and tallow trade drew men connected with it to California, and it increased the number of ships along the coast. The

---

106. Cited in Ogden, Sea Otter Trade, p. 33.
107. Bancroft, Calif., I, 540.
108. Bancroft, Calif., II, 272.
109. Ibid., I, 272.
110. Ibid., II, 272.
111. Ibid., II, 303.
112. Ibid., II, 653-654.

The strangers, once admitted, were usually received with typical California hospitality, and the aid and kindness which overland parties
received in later years, at the end of their long journeys has frequently
been told.

All foreigners coming to California were, theoretically, required
to have passports, issued by a Mexican official, approving their entry
into the province. This requirement was seldom fulfilled. Obviously,
deserters and sick sailors left by their ships were not able to comply
with this provision. In later years the groups of Americans coming
overland made no attempts to obtain permission to enter California. The
way for them, in this respect, had been made easy by earlier settlers.

In 1841 General Vallejo received orders from the Minister of War in
Mexico that no foreign immigrant who had not received a legal passport
was to be permitted to remain. Yet when the Bartleson Party and the
Workman-Rowland Company arrived that year, they were aided in securing
these documents. In his report to the central government Vallejo stated
that he "had employed the only means to reconcile justice with circumstances and duty with prudence, the country having the dire alternative
of consenting to what it cannot prevent, or commanding without being able
to enforce, for want of military strength."[113] The foreign element had
become too strong. To legalize matters,[114] passports could be obtained
by the newcomers after they arrived in California, and permits to travel,
marry, take up residence, or to become naturalized citizens, could
usually be obtained with little difficulty.[115]

b. INTEGRATION OF FOREIGNERS INTO THE COMMUNITY

Once legally accepted in California the foreigners were soon inte-
grated into the community. Says one prominent observer,

It is interesting and sometimes amusing to see how soon these
first pioneers became thorough-going Spaniards -- adopting
the religion, language, manners and customs of their new
friends. Correspondence was carried on in Spanish, even between English-speaking persons.[116]

Being few in numbers and spread throughout the province, there was
little possibility for the non-Spanish white people to live by themselves.
They appeared willing to take up the California way of life with little
hesitancy, and apparently were wise in doing so. William Heath Davis

---

113. Cardinal Goodwin, "Foreigners in California Before 1842-
II," _Overland_, May, 1912, p. 416.
114. T. J. Farnham, _Life, Adventures, and Travels in California_
(New York, 1849), pp. 56-57; Dawson, _op. cit._, p. 36.
115. Bancroft, _Calif._, III, 175-180.
116. Sanchez, _op. cit._, p. 135.

writes, "The native Californians were about the happiest and contented people I ever saw, as also were the early foreigners who settled among them and intermarried with them, adopted their habits and customs, and became, as it were, a part of themselves."[117] In later years, however, when the proportion of foreigners was increased rapidly by overland immigration, there appeared more of a split between the Californians and the Anglo-Americans.

The first step in the process of integration was the entrance of the newcomers into the economic life of California. This was accomplished without great difficulty because this backward province had need of all kinds of trained or experienced people. A sailor on a sailing vessel was a "jack-of-all-trades," and sailors who deserted helped to make up the deficiency in artisans.

> ...A sailor would occasionally desert, and settle among the rancheros; if a good man, industrious, and willing to work, especially if he had some mechanical skill at carpentry or other useful industry, he was encouraged by the rancheros to stay, and was treated with kindness; but if indolent and worthless fellows deserted, while kindly treated, they were not encouraged to remain but were presented with horses and perhaps some clothes, and persuaded to ride away to some other rancho.[118]

The sailors became carpenters, masons, coopers, smiths, millers, and sawyers. This tendency is illustrated by a summary of the occupations of the thirteen foreign residents of 1820.

Jose Bolcof	Portuguese	shoemaker, later landowner
Daniel Call	American	carpenter
Joseph Chapman	American	carpenter, blacksmith, and miller
Bob Cristobal	Negro of un-determined nationality	no information
Thomas Doak	American	carpenter
Fisher	Negro	no information
John Gilroy	Scotch	cooper, soap maker, milwright
Thomas Lester	English	no information
John Mulligan	Irish	taught weaving to Indians
Pascual	Negro	no information
Antonio Rocha	Portuguese	no information
John Rose	Scotch	drummer and mender of drums
Ignacio Thomas	English	no information, blind

---

117. Davis, op. cit., p. 67.
118. Davis, op. cit., p. 155.

In the twenties came the first of the business men who were almost completely to dominate the foreign and domestic commerce of California, a field which the natives had not and did not care to enter. The merchants, therefore, also filled a vital need in the economic life of the province. They were cordially received and became respected members of the community. Foreigners can also be found practicing medicine, teaching, manning vessels engaged in local trade, operating ranchos, and acting as officials. In general it might be said that the foreigners were useful and energetic members of the society.

Turning from the economic to the religious problems, we find a similar amalgamation taking place. California at this time was strictly a Roman Catholic country. As in all Spanish colonies, the Church was strong, and uniformity in religion was considered necessary for political unity. The padres were unbending in religious matters. "...McCulloch wrote that he and Hartnell had compromised the matter satisfactorily by consenting to remove their hats and go on their knees on certain occasions."[119] But the sailors had little objection to becoming Catholics. As Dana says, "...American and English, who intend to reside here, become Papists, -- the current phrase among them being, 'a man must leave his conscience at Cape Horn.'"[120]

Aside from purely religious considerations the reasons that most foreigners allowed themselves to be converted are apparent. A non-Catholic could not marry, nor could he own land, nor could he become a citizen. In fact according to the law, a non-Catholic was not to be permitted to remain in the country more than a few weeks, but, as most Mexican laws, this regulation was not rigidly enforced. A few stalwarts held out, but to do so meant that (1) a man did not intend to marry one the native girls (Anglo-Saxon women were very rare before the overland route was opened up around 1840) and (2) he did not intend to shift his political allegiance to California. In a place and a time that was filled with rumors of foreign aggression the implication often followed that the individual in question expected California to be annexed by his own Protestant country. Thomas Larkin, who became the United States consul at Monterey, and Nathan Spears were two who fulfilled both of these conditions.

When he was baptized, as part of the ceremony, a foreigner received a Spanish name, or had his own Hispanicized. This custom had a greater social than a religious significance for it aided the process of amalgamation. Don Alfredo was more a part of the California scene than Alfred Robinson; Don Juan Bautista more a Californian than John Cooper. Henry Delane Fitch was baptized as Enrique Domingo Fitch. James

---

119. Bancroft, Calif., II, 479.
120. Dana, op. cit., p. 99.

Alexander Forbes was known as Don Diego, and John Gilroy was baptized as Juan Antonio Maria Gilroy. Even those who were not baptized were known by Spanish equivalents of their names; Thomas Larkin, for instance, was called Don Tomas.

Probably even more important in bringing the outsiders into the community life was their marriage to California girls. Nearly all of the men who came to California in the early period were single, adventurers with few home ties. The very fact that they took up residence in this far away land indicates that their attachment to their native country was not strong. Obviously women could not get to California on the exploring ships, men-of-war, whalers, or sea otter hunters that brought most of the men, although one or two came on trading ships. If the sailors, merchants, or young clerks had girls or wives in other ports, they were content to forget about them.

On the other hand marriage to a _hija del pais_ was not to be shunned. The young ladies of California were exceptionally gifted representatives of their sex, often beautiful girls with lovely figures.[121] Not only were they physically attractive, but they embodied the grace, gaiety, and poise common to natives of both sexes.[122] In addition they were fine homemakers, having been trained in domestic pursuits from childhood.[123] Another factor in their favor, at least from the outsiders point of view, was their seeming preference for non-Californian husbands. Mofras, a French diplomatic observer, stated: "Among 6,000 white inhabitants /in 1841/ there are perhaps 600 foreigners, whom the women prefer to their own countrymen, for they are usually more industrious, treat them more considerately, and take better care of their children."[124] Foreigners thus had little difficulty in assuming the blessings of matrimony if they so desired. However, the young men of native birth were not at all pleased by this turn of events.[125] One of the most biased observers offers this as one of the reasons that a group of Americans and Englishmen were forcibly exiled in 1840.[126]

At any rate many Americans and Englishmen were soon allied with the leading native families. Alfred Robinson married Ana Maria, daughter of Captain Jose de la Guerra y Noriega. Henry Dalton's ladylove was Guadalupe Zamorano, daughter of Don Augustin Vicente Zamorano. Abel Stearns married Arcadia Bandini. William Heath Davis took to wife Maria Jesus, daughter of Don Joaquin Estudillo, Jacob Leese married Rosalia Vallejo, sister of General Mariano G. Vallejo, the most wealthy and

---

121. Bryant, _op. cit._, p. 261; Lyman, _op. cit._, p. 210, 213; Robinson, _op. cit._, pp. 33-34; Sanchez, _op. cit._, p. 133.
122. Dana, _op. cit._, p. 97.
123. Davis, _op. cit._, pp. 60-61.
124. Mofras, _op. cit._, II, 12.
125. Mittell cited in Sanchez, _op. cit._, pp. 134-135.
126. Farnham, _op. cit._

influential citizen in California,[127] and John Cooper married Encarnacion Vallejo, another sister of General Vallejo. William A. Richardson married Maria Antonia Martinez, daughter of the Commandant of the San Francisco Presidio.[128] The list can be multiplied almost indefinitely.

Besides taking unto themselves native wives, the Anglo-Americans were not slow in accepting the customs of their adopted country. In the conduct of their business and social relation with the Californians it was, of course, necessary for them to use the language of the land, and, in some cases, their wives could not speak English. It was not unusual for the newcomers to wear Spanish clothes.[129] The most prominent merchants, however, continued to dress in the European manner -- perhaps to their disadvantage.[130] Dana gives the following picture of Alfred Robinson at the latter's wedding. "Our agent /Robinson/, with a tight, black, swallow-tailed coat just imported from Boston, a high stiff cravat, looking as if he had been pinned and skewered, with only his feet and hands left free, took the floor..."[131]

The home life of foreigners married to native women quite naturally followed the traditions of the wife's country. The meals, for example, were Mexican meals. We have the testimony of one visitor that he was not overly impressed by this arrangement. After describing a meal consisting mainly of beans covered with a hot sauce, Sir George Simpson, governor-general of the Hudson's Bay Company, continued, "When to the foregoing sketch are added bad tea and worse wine, the reader has picked up a perfect idea of Californian breakfast, Californian dinner, and Californian supper, and is quite able to estimate the sacrifice which a naturalized John Bull makes for the pleasures of matrimony and the comforts of Roman Catholicism."[132]

The children that resulted from these unions were raised as Mexican children. In most cases they were given Spanish names, spoke only the Spanish language, and absorbed the customs and usuages of the predominately Spanish community.[133] It was apparently a successful process, and there was little evidence of the moral disintegration frequently found in the children whose parents represent different cultural and racial backgrounds.[134]

---

127. Davis, op. cit., p. 30.
128. Ibid., p. 10.
129. Dana, op. cit., p. 87.
130. Mofras, op. cit., II, 14-15.
131. Dana, op. cit., p. 396.
132. Simpson, op. cit., 311-312.
133. Dana, op. cit., p. 100, 216.
134. Says Davis, "The intermarriage of the foreigners in early times with the Californians produced a fine race of children, who partook of the characteristics of both parents. The stock, as usual, was improved by the mingling of the different nationalities." Davis, op. cit., p. 125.

c. POLITICAL INFLUENCE OF THE FOREIGNERS

The foreign inhabitants participated in the political as well as in the economic life of California and exerted an influence out of all portion to their relative numerical strength. In the periodic revolutions which punctuated California's history under Mexican rule, they took a conspicuous part. The foreigners also played an important role in the events of 1846 which led to annexation by the United States. In that year Fremont's defiance of Mexican authority had caused the more recent immigrants to rise in the Bear Flag Revolt. The Mexican War, of which the Californians learned a short time later, soon overshadowed this internal rebellion, and the foreigners rendered valuable assistance to the United States military leaders in California. Even had Fremont's aggressive actions, the Bear Flag Revolt, and the Mexican War not intervened, it is probable that the non-Spanish residents would have attained peacefully California's independence within a short time.[135]

---

135. Cleland, Wilderness, p. 204.

CHAPTER III

THE BRITISH PIONEERS

1. INTRODUCTION

At the opening of the fateful year, 1846, there were approximately
680 men of non-Spanish and non-Mexican birth living in California. Of
course, a much greater number of foreigners had reached California, but
some of them had been only casual visitors, others had moved away after
residences of various lengths of time, and still others had died there.
Since Gilroy had arrived in 1814, the numbers of foreign residents had
increased to thirteen in 1820, approximately one hundred and fifty in
1830, and three hundred and eighty in 1840.

Of the thirteen foreigners of 1820, five were men of British birth,
Gilroy and Rose being Scotchmen, Lester and Thomas Englishmen, and
Mulligan an Irishman. Of the other eight, three were Americans, one a
Russian, one a Portuguese, and three were negroes of undetermined
nationality.[1]

Of the one hundred and forty-six foreigners of 1830 which Bancroft
lists, at least sixty were of British birth.[2] There were sixteen
Irishmen, sixteen Scotchmen, and twenty-eight Englishmen. Fifty-two
of the remainder were from the United States, while the rest represented various nationalities or were men whose nationality cannot be
determined.

It is apparent that in the first period in which foreign immigration into California was permitted -- at least until 1830 -- Britishers
were the predominant element, even overshadowing the Americans. This
numerical supremacy was lost during the 1830's as American ships and men
came to dominate the hide and tallow trade, which accounted for the
immigration of many California pioneers. Perhaps even more important
was the rapid increase of overland immigration of trappers in the late
1830's and settlers in the early 1840's, for quite naturally, citizens
of the United States made up most of the transcontinental parties. By
the time of the Bear Flag Revolt and the Mexican War, the number of
Americans in California was much greater than the number of Britishers.

Citizens of Great Britain came to California in many ways and for
various reasons. At no time was there any concerted movement of English
families into California, looking for a new place to establish homes, as
there was to the United States, Canada, Australia, New Zealand, and
South Africa. This period was one of imperial apathy in Great Britain,
in which the "Little Englanders" had caused most of their countrymen to
question the value of colonies and in which no government support of

---

1. Bancroft, Calif., II, 308.
2. Ibid., II, 681-682.

colonization could be expected.

Emigration to California from the British Isles was not only on a small scale but completely haphazard. In spite of the disillusionment in colonial enterprises which followed the loss of the thirteen American colonies in 1783, and which lasted up until the 1870's, emigration to the United States and Canada continued, and British settlers commenced their movement into South Africa and Australia. California was not included in this migration because it was not under the British flag, as were the future dominions, and because it did not have the historical, cultural, and economic connections with Great Britain that the United States had.

It has been said that the three C's of colonization have been commerce, conquest, and conversion. Of these three the only one that had any significance from the British standpoint in California was commerce. Conquest was ruled out by Great Britain's official policy, at this time, of indifference toward colonial acquisitions. Conversion played no part -- except perhaps in a reverse direction. California was a settled country, and one in which the Roman Catholic Church was supreme and unquestioned. Instead of English missionaries converting heathens, Englishmen were converted from Protestantism to Catholicism. Commerce, on the other hand, was instrumental in drawing to California the British traders and sailors who eventually settled there.

2. JOURNEYING TO CALIFORNIA -- SAILORS AND OVERLAND IMMIGRANTS

British sailors came to California not only on British ships but on ships flying many different flags. Crews of most ships were cosmopolitan, enrolling men of various nationalities in their number.[3] Dana lists twelve or fifteen nationalities represented at the hide-curing station in San Diego, from ships of only three or four different countries. He continued,

> The night before the vessels were ready to sail, all the
> Europeans united and had an entertainment at the Rosa's
> hide-house, and we had songs of every nation and tongue.
> A German gave us "Ach! mein lieber Augustin!", the three
> Frenchmen roared through the Marseilles Hymn, the English
> and Scotchmen gave us "Rule, Britannia", and "Wha'll be
> King but Charlie?", the Italians and Spaniards screamed
> through some national affairs, for which I was none the
> wise, and the three Yankees made an attempt at the "Star-
> spangled Banner". After these national tributes had been
> paid, the Austrian gave us a pretty little love-song, and
> the Frenchmen sang a spirited thing -- "Sentinelle! O

---

3. Dana, op. cit., p. 112, 153.

prenez garde a vous!" -- and then followed the melange which might have been expected.[4]

A few men of British nationality came overland, in spite of the great predominance of Americans in the transcontinental parties. The frontiersmen of the United States were usually from families which had lived in America for one or more generations as the new immigrants normally settled, at least temporarily, in the partially civilized East. However, among the members of the ill-fated Donner Party are found James F. Reed, born in Ireland; Patrick Breen, his wife, Peggy, and their children, all of whom, except for the youngest children were of Irish birth; the Irishman Patrick Dolan; and John Denton, an Englishman.[5] The Stevens Party of 1844 included the Irishmen Edmund Bray, Patrick Martin, James Miller, Martin Murphy, and John Sullivan. Two more Irishmen, George Davis and William Northgrave, came by land from Oregon in the Hastings Party of 1843 and the McMahon-Clymer Party of 1845 respectively. In the Grigsby-Ide Party of 1845 were the Englishmen Henry Marshall, John Marshall, and James Gregson. Undoubtedly many other Britishers, such as Charles and Jonathan Parr, came overland in unnamed parties or in parties whose muster lists are not recorded.

a. BRITISH SEA CAPTAINS -- COOPER, SCOTT, SNOOK, AND WILSON

A group of prominent British pioneers came to California as captains of ships engaged in the hide and tallow trade and decided to make their homes in California. In this number were captains Cooper, Scott, Snook, and Wilson.

Captain James Scott and Captain John Wilson, both residents of Santa Barbara, became partners in mercantile ventures, ship owning, sea otter hunting, and stock raising, the partnership lasting from 1839 to 1847. James Scott, a native of Scotland, first visited California in 1826 as supercargo of the Olive Branch and later of the Waverly. In the years 1827-1828 he was master of the Huascar. Although he was constantly on the move, serving as captain and supercargo on several other vessels, he considered Santa Barbara his home.[6]

Captain John Wilson also came to California in 1826. He served as captain of various ships that sailed the coastal waters -- Thomas Nowlan, 1828; Ayacucho, 1831-1837; Index, 1838-1839; 1841-1843; Fly, 1840; and Juanita, 1844-1845.[7] Captain Wilson and his ship the Ayacucho appear frequently in Two Years Before the Mast. Wilson is described as follows:

He was a short, active, well-built man about fifty years of

---

4. Dana, op. cit., p. 153.
5. George R. Stewart, Jr., Ordeal by Hunger; The Story of the Donner Party (New York, 1936), p. 14, 25.
6. Bancroft, Calif., V, 714.
7. Ibid., V, 777.

age /in 1835/; and being some twenty years older than our captain, and a thorough seaman, he did not hesitate to give his advice, and from giving advice he gradually came to taking the command....Wilson was a kind man, and had an encouraging and pleasant way of speaking to us, which made everything go easily.[8]

Sometime before 1836 the Captain married Romona Carrillo de Pacheco,[9] widow of Ramouldo Pacheco, who had been killed in the battle between Victoria's and Echaendia's forces near Cahuenga on December 5, 1831. She was described by Simpson as "...one of the prettiest and most agreeable women that we had ever met either here or elsewhere."[10]

The two partners were apparently successful business men as Scott was described as "...one of the most prosperous merchants in the country..."[11] In addition they were extensive property owners having been granted the ranchos Canada de los Osos and Pecho y Yslai on September 24, 1845 and Rancho Canada del Chorro on October 10, 1845. The former ranchos totalled 34,430.70 acres and the latter 3,166.99 acres. In that same year the partners, with James McKinley, bought the San Luis Obispo Mission and its remaining lands for $510. Scott died in 1851, and Wilson, retiring from the sea after the American conquest to live the life of a prosperous ranchero, died in 1861.

Joseph Francisco Snook was another English sea captain who settled in California. He came to California as the master of the Ayacucho around 1830 and continued to follow the sea after taking up his residence in the provinces. He served as captain of the following ships in later years: Catalina, 1833-1839; Jovan Quipuzcoana, 1840-1842; and Juanita, 1846. As captain of the Jovan Quipuzcoana he transported the Graham party to San Blas when they were arrested and exiled in 1840.[12]

Snook was naturalized in 1833 and a short while later married to Maria Antonia Alvardo. Besides his sea-faring activities he also served as a trader and as a land owner. On June 8, 1839, he was granted the Rancho Tamalas, and on February 16, 1842, the Rancho San Bernardo which embraced four square leagues in San Diego County. He later moved with his family to this property and spent the rest of his life there.[13]

---

8. Dana, op. cit., pp. 91-92.
9. George L. Hardin, Don Agustin V. Zamorano, Statesman, Soldier, Craftsman, and California's First Printer (Los Angeles, 1934), p. 68.
10. Simpson, op. cit., I, 376.
11. Ibid., See also Herman Leader, "A Voyage from the Columbia to California in 1840 from the Hournal of Sir James Douglas," California Historical Society Quarterly, VIII, 106.
12. Davis, op. cit., p. 47.
13. Bancroft, Calif., V, 726.

There were few men in California more widely known or better liked than Captain John Roger Cooper, or Juan Bautista Roger Cooper, as he was baptized. He was born in the Alderney Islands and came as a boy to the United States with his mother, who by a second marriage became the mother of Thomas O. Larkin. Cooper first saw California in 1823. In 1826 he sold his ship, the Rover, to Governor Arguello, but continued to act as its skipper. He was baptized in 1827 and in that same year married to Encarnacion Vallejo, sister of General Mariano Vallejo. It was for his bride that he built the Cooper adobe on what is now the southwest corner of Polk and Munros Streets in Monterey.

Cooper later commanded other vessels, including the state owned ship California, the local navy.[14] When Commodore Jones of the United States Navy seized Monterey in 1842, the California "commander-in-chief" is said to have rushed out of doors (being ashore at the time) and to have declaimed, "Well, I wouldn't care a snap for the loss of the old schooner, if I had only got a well-rope out of her first."[15] Although in this Cooper was not adhering to the accepted standard for such incidents, he was at least living up to the traditions of the California navy.

In common with most of the prominent men in California, he had several financial interests. Cooper was one of the outstanding merchants of the coast. Abel Stearns entered business life in California as one of his travelling agents,[16] and James McKinley at one time occupied a similar position. In 1833 he was licensed to hunt sea otters. Cooper also became one of the biggest land owners, being granted the Rancho El Molino in 1836, and having purchased Rancho El Sur from Juan B. Alvarado and the Rancho Bolses del Potrero y Moro Cojo for $2,000 from Joaquin de la Torre. Rancho El Molino contained ten and one-half square leagues in Sonoma County, while each of the others, located in Monterey County, were of two square leagues. After giving up the sea permanently in 1850, he divided his time between Monterey and his ranchos. He died in San Francisco in the year 1872.[17]

3. BRITISH MERCHANTS -- SPENCE, WATSON, MC KINLEY[18]

Once having settled in California the Anglo-Saxons engaged in various

---

14. Simpson, op. cit., I, 358.
15. Phelps, op. cit., pp. 244-245.
16. Sanchez, op. cit., p. 142.
17. Bancroft, Calif., II, 766.
18. The division of the British pioneers into groups on the basis of vocation is to some extent an arbitrary matter. Many of these men could be placed in two or more different categories. Each of the four sea captains mentioned above were land holders, and each had trading interests. Several of those that are listed under rancheros were also merchants. Even the doctors had their ranchos and, in some cases, engaged in mercantile activities.

occupations. Because of their superior education and training, the lack of caste restrictions on their occupations, and their greater industry, the Britishers and Americans, in many cases, became important members of the community. They dominated the commercial life of the country, supplied most of the skilled labor, were looked upon for medical aid, and became important rancheros.

The big merchants of California were mostly Americans and Britishers. In the San Francisco Bay area William A. Richardson and the Americans Jacob Lesse and William Heath Davis were the most important. The Hudson's Bay Company's post in Yerba Buena under its manager, William Glen Rae, handled a large share of the wholesale trade of the Bay region during its brief life. In San Jose, James Alexander Forbes, a prominent British merchant, acted as local agent for the Hudson's Bay Company.

Although the American Abel Stearns was the outstanding merchant in Los Angeles, several men of British birth were engaged in business activities there for varying lengths of time. Among these we find Hugo Ried, John Forster, and James Johnston. The Scotch sea captains, John Wilson and James Scott, conducted their trading operations in Santa Barbara. When Mofras visited San Diego in 1841, he wrote that of the twenty houses there the most pretentious belonged to Englishmen and American, who controlled all the commerce.[19] The English merchants in that village were Joseph Snook and Edward Stokes. In Monterey the important British merchants were W. E. P. Hartnell, J. B. R. Cooper, David Spence, James Watson, and James McKinley.[20]

Spence, one of the leading businessmen of California, was a native of Scotland. He came to Monterey in 1824 after having lived for several years in South America. John Begg and Company, of which McCulloch, Hartnell and Company was the Monterey branch, made a contract with the Peruvian government to supply it with salt beef. Spence was sent to California, with a number of salters and coopers, to superintend the meat packing activities,[21] which were to be conducted near Monterey. Various difficulties made this enterprise unsuccessful, but in 1827 Spence went into business for himself and prospered from the beginning,[22] having all the attributes of a good business man. Colton describes him as "...a man of unblemished integrity and sterling sense..."[23]

He was baptized in 1827 at Santa Cruz as David Estevan Spence and, two years later, married the "pretty and lively" Adelaida Estrada. In 1830 he became a naturalized citizen of Mexico.

---

19. Mofras, op. cit., I, 171.
20. Davis, op. cit., p. 2; Mofras, op. cit., I, 214.
21. Bancroft, Calif., II, 519-520.
22. Simpson, op. cit., I, 347-348.
23. Colton, op. cit., p. 422.

Spence took a greater part in political affairs in California than did most foreigners. During the Solis revolt he was active in organizing the defense of the capitol. In 1836 he became a member of the diputacion and a secret supporter of the Alvarado Administration. He was elector and justice of the peace in 1839 and 1840, member of the departmental junta 1843 to 1845, and in 1845 leader of the company of foreigners which was organized to protect Monterey during the Micheltorena troubles. In the troubled year 1846, most people believed that he was trying to promote an English protectorate, although Thomas Larkin, the American consul, regarded him as friendly to the United States. After the change of flags, he served in several different local political posts.

Besides his commercial and political activities, Spence was also a large land owner. He was the grantee of Rancho Encinal y Buena Esperanza, comprising two square leagues granted in 1834 and a third granted in 1839. In 1848 he gave up his business affairs completely and devoted his time and energy to stock raising, owning approximately 4,000 head of cattle and 500 horses.[24] Spence died in 1875 at the age of 73.

> Don David had an excellent reputation among the pioneers of Cal.,
> few exerting so wide and good an influence. While not exactly
> popular by reason of his conservatism and closeness in money
> matters, obstinate as any of his race, and making enemies as
> well as friends, he yet merited and received the respect of all
> classes.[25]

James Watson, another merchant of Monterey, was an English sailor who came to California around 1824. He married Mariana Escamillo and, by the time that he became a naturalized citizen in 1836, had four children. In Monterey, Watson became a respected citizen, taking part in local political affairs, and a prominent and wealthy merchant.[26] He purchased the Rancho San Benito, of one and one-half square leagues in Monterey County, which had originally been granted to Francisco Garcia. After the American conquest, his title was upheld by the United States Land Commission. On his rancho Watson grazed 2,000 cattle, 1,000 sheep, and 100 horses,[27] but he was ruined by the drought of 1863 and died that same year.[28]

James McKinley maintained a good reputation throughout his long business career in California. Coming from Cardrops, in Renfrewshire, Scotland, McKinley was left as a boy in San Francisco or Santa Barbara

---

24. Davis, op. cit., p. 390.
25. Bancroft, Calif., V. 731.
26. Mofras, op. cit., I, 214.
27. Davis, op. cit., p. 390.
28. Bancroft, Calif., V, 769.

by a whaling ship in 1824. During the thirties he travelled much of the time, acting as agent for Cooper and Larkin, but eventually entered business for himself. At one time he was owner of the schooner _Ayacucho_, one of the most familiar vessels in California waters. In 1844 and 1845 he played a leading part in the movement of the foreign residents against Micheltorena. For a brief period he was in partnership with Hugo Reid and at a later date with Henry Fitch and Henry Paty.

McKinley purchased from Martin Kolivera and Vicente Feliz the Rancho Moro y Cayucos, which encompassed two square leagues in San Luis Obispo County. During Pio Pico's governorship, with John Forster he bought the Mission San Juan Capistrano and its remaining property for $710 and with Scott and Wilson, the Mission San Luis Obispo for $510.[29]

Little is known about McKinley's activities after the American conquest other than that he was married in 1848 to Carmen Amesti and that he died in 1876.[30]

In the late thirties and early forties, as men from the United States came to dominate the foreign population of California, they also came to dominate its commerce. In 1841 Sir George Simpson could report, "...the trade of the bay /San Francisco/, and in fact, of the whole province, is entirely in the hands of foreigners, who are almost exclusively of the English race. Of that race, however, the Americans are considerably more numerous than the former."[31]

4.   BRITISH DOCTORS -- BALE, N. A. DEN, R. S. DEN, STOKES

The foreigners also filled the province's need for doctors. In fact, the natives looked upon any foreigner as an authority on medical matters. Said one pioneer, "I know not why, but an Anglo-Saxon is synonymous with an M.D. Many an extranjero who never before possessed sufficient confidence in himself to administer even a dose of Epsom, after killing God knows how many, has at length become a tolerable empiric. One thing in favor of the sick is, that after a lapse of years the greatest part of the drugs lose their virtue."[32] Aside from the everyday doctoring that all foreigners were required to do, we find several Britishers performing medical duties.

Edward T. Bale, the first Anglo-Saxon physician in Monterey, was described as "...a man of good education but quarrelsome."[33] Sir James Douglas of the Hudson's Bay Company met Bale in 1840 but was not impressed by the Doctor's character or veracity.[34] He was born in London in the

29.   Dakin, _op. cit._, p. 130.
30.   Bancroft, _Calif._, IV, 725.
31.   Simpson, _op. cit._, I, 292-293.
32.   Dakin, _op. cit._, p. 13.
33.   Sanchez, _op. cit._, p. 258.
34.   Leader, "A Voyage," _Loc. cit._, VIII, 100.

year 1811. After completing his medical education, Bale was commissioned surgeon on the English ship Harriet. This ship arrived in Monterey in 1837, having sailed around Cape Horn. How he secured his release from naval duties is unknown, but he became a permanent resident of California and soon married Maria Ignacia Soberanes. From 1840 to 1843, by General Vallejo's appointment, he served as surgeon of the California forces, the only Anglo-Saxon who ever occupied that position.[35]

It was Bale's misfortune to have his destiny linked with the Vallejo family. On the occasion of Sir George Simpson's visit to General Mariano Vallejo, perhaps then the most powerful man in California, the General was confined to his bed. He had injured his hip slightly in a riding accident, but the injury was aggravated by Bale's treatment. As Simpson describes the incident, "he /Vallejo/, sent a messenger to the only practicioner in San Francisco, one Bail /sic/ from Manchester /?/, for a strengthening plaster; the doctor, who sometimes takes doses very different from those he prescribes, sent by mistake a blister of cantharides, which being supposed to be salutary in proportion to the pain of its application, was allowed to work double duties on the poor general's bruise..."[36]

After moving from Monterey to Sonoma, Bale again became involved with the Vallejos. His wife, Maria, was a niece of Salvador Vallejo, the General's brother. The story goes that the doctor, being of very jealous temperament, became angry at the affection displayed by the young lady towards her uncle. As a result he challenged Don Salvador to a duel, but in so doing made the mistake of pitting himself against the best swordsman in California. Bale was not only soundly trounced but thoroughly humilated when Don Salvador, using his sword as whip, gave him a threshing. Bale determined upon revenge. One summer day he saw Don Salvador crossing the street, and approaching from behind, fired two shots at him, one of them grazing the neck. Bale was later seized by a group of the Vallejo Indians who were out to revenge Don Salvador. As the doctor was being lead towards a large oak, known as "The Punishment Tree," General Mariano Vallejo intervened, insisting upon a trial. Ultimately, Governor Micheltorena ordered Bale released, possibly fearing trouble with England if punishment was inflicted. General Vallejo directed him to leave Sonoma.[37]

This episode was not enough to keep a good man down, however, and Dr. Bale became a pillar of the community. On March 14, 1841, he was

---

35. G. D. Lyman, "The Scapel Under Three Flags in California," California Historical Society Quarterly, IV, 153-154.
36. Simpson, op. cit., I, 316.
37. Myrtle M. McKittrick, Vallejo Son of California (Portland, Oregon, 1944), p. 227.

granted four square leagues of land in Napa County known as Rancho Carne Humana. On this site the present cities of Calistoga and St. Helena are located. Not only did he improve this land but, after settling in St. Helena, amazed the natives by his energy in building a grist mill and a saw mill.[38] The grist mill is still preserved as one of the landmarks of Napa County.[39]

Dr. Bale journeyed to the mines in 1849 but soon returned to St. Helena, where he died in October of that year.[40] A fellow pioneer says of him, "Bale was considered a scientific and talented man in his profession as physician and surgeon by the early men of California."[41]

George Allen served on occasion as surgeon and dentist, in addition to his primary activities as a trader and a politician.[42] Born in Ireland of Scotch-English parentage, he landed in Monterey in 1822. In 1824 he was baptized as Josef Jorge Tomas at San Carlos and two years later married to Petra Bordonda. Stephen Anderson, a Scotch trader, acted as a physician upon occasion during the period from 1828 to 1832 that he was in California.[43] In 1846 William McKee, a Scotch physician, arrived at Monterey and commenced his practice. He later engaged in trade and also became a landholder.[44]

Nicholas Augustus Den, an Irish physician, lived in Santa Barbara, having arrived in that port in 1836 on the ship Kent. He had studied medicine at the University of Dublin but did not graduate. Although Dr. Den avoided acquiring a practice, he never refused to answer a call for help, nor did he exact a fee. He was considered particularly adept as a phlebotomist.[45]

His primary interest was in stock raising, but he served as collector of the port in 1842 and alcalde in 1845. On April 30, 1840, he was granted the Rancho Los dos Pueblos, which embraced approximately three square leagues in Santa Barbara County. In 1840 with his father-in-law, Daniel Hill, he leased the Santa Barbara Mission for $1200 per year and continued to lease it after the Mission was sold to his brother, Richard S. Den, in 1846. Just before the American conquest Governor Pio Pico granted him Rancho San Marcos, eight square leagues in Santa Barbara

---

38. An Illustrated History of Sonoma County, California (Chicago, 1889), p. 703.

39. Joseph R. Knowland, California, A Landmark History. Story of the Preservation and Marking of Early Day Shrines (Oakland, California, 1941), pp. 193-194.

40. Lyman, "Scapel," loc. cit., IV, 153-154.

41. Davis, op. cit., p. 137.

42. Bancroft, Calif., II, 690.

43. Ibid., II, 697.

44. Bancroft, Calif., IV, 724.

45. Lyman, "Scapel," loc. cit., IV, 157.

county.

Although of unprepossessing appearance, he was "...an intelligent, educated and accomplished gentleman, and much liked."[46] Bancroft adds, "Dr. Den is said to have been of good family, and became in Cal. a most popular stock-raiser of considerable wealth and an excellent reputation."[47]

Richard Somerset Den, brother of Nicholas, also became one of California's early doctors. He was born in County Killenny, Ireland in 1821. After preliminary schooling in Dublin and training in a local hospital, he was awarded his first medical certificate from the School of Anatomy, Medicine, and Surgery in Dublin and two years later received his final qualifications. Through the aid of Sir John Pirie, Lord Mayor of London, he obtained a position as surgeon on the ship Glenswilly, on which he sailed to Melbourne, Australia, thence to Valparaiso, and finally to Mazatlan. There he received news that his brother was in Santa Barbara. Resigning his position on the Glenswilly, he sailed for California, and after the reunion with his brother, finally settled in Los Angeles.[48]

During the Mexican War Don Ricardo served as Chief Physician and Surgeon of the Mexican forces in southern California.[49] At the time of the Gold Rush he went for a short period to the mines where his practice brought him up to $1,000 a day.[50]

On June 10, 1846, Pio Pico granted Dr. Den the Santa Barbara Mission and its remaining grounds, but the American courts later ruled that Pico had no right to sell church property, and the mission reverted to the Franciscans.

The great faith which the Spanish people had in his ability was expressed in the saying, "Despues de Dios, Doctor Don Ricardo" ("After God, Dr. Richard"). One pioneer has left the following picture of him,

He was seldom seen except on horseback, in which fashion he visited his patients, and was, all in all, somewhat a man of mystery. He rode a magnificent coal-black charger, and was himself always dressed in black. He wore, too, a black felt hat; and beneath the hat there clustered a mass of wavy hair as white as snow. In addition to all this, his collar was so high that he was compelled to hold his head erect;

---

46. Davis, op. cit., p. 123.
47. Bancroft, Calif., II, 779.
48. An Illustrated History of Los Angeles County California (Chicago, 1889), pp. 197-198.
49. Ibid., p. 198.
50. Lyman, "Scapel," loc. cit., IV, 165.

and as if to offset the immaculate linen, he tied around the collar a large black-silk scarf. Thus attired and seated on his richly-caparisoned horse, Dr. Den appeared always dignified, and even imposing.[51]

James Stokes, "merchant, farmer, and doctor," was one of California's all around men. As an English sailor, he came to Monterey around 1834 and soon took up the duties of a druggist and physician. He had been a hospital steward and brought ashore with him a medicine sea chest fitted out with apothecary scales, a little store of medicine, and a doctor's book.[52] "Medicine was not then a regulated profession. Anyone who could roll a pill, or administer 'draps' not only could, but did, hang out a shingle in California".[53]

In the late thirties Stokes built the Stokes-Gragg adobe, a landmark in Monterey, located on Hartnell Street, described as one of the finest salas in the capitol. When affairs of state were to be held, the Stokes house was often pressed into service.[54] In 1844 Dr. Stokes brought his bride, Maria Josefa Soto, to the new house.

Besides his medical activities, Stokes kept a store in Monterey and operated a cattle ranch. Some time before the American conquest, he acquired title to the Rancho de los Verjeles, on which he grazed 2,200 cattle and 100 horses.[55] However, at a later date his claim was rejected by the United States Land Commission.[56] In the affairs of 1846 he was considered as having supported plans for an English protectorate, but he was the first to raise the United States flag at San Jose, where he served for a brief time as alcalde.[57] In later years Stokes drops completely from view.

5. BRITISH RANCHEROS -- DAWSON, MC INTOSH, BLACK, MURPHY, FOXEN, REID, WORKMAN, FORSTER, STOKES.

A large number of British immigrants also entered the basic industry of the country as rancheros and farmers, in addition to the grantees mentioned above. William Welch was granted Rancho Las Juntas, three square leagues in Contra Costa County, in 1844. The city of Martinez is now located on this site. John Martin a Scotch sailor, acquired the

---

51. Harris Newmark, Sixty Years in Southern California, 1853-1913 Containing the Reminiscences of Harris Newmark (New York, 1926, pp. 108-109.

52. Lyman, "Scapel," loc. cit., IV, 156.

53. Laura Bride Powers, Old Monterey California's Adobe Capitol (San Francisco, 1934), p. 256.

54. Ibid.

55. Davis, op. cit., p. 391.

56. Hoffman, op. cit., Index Number 169.

57. Bancroft, Calif., V, 735-736.

Rancho Corte de Madera de Novato in Marin County.[58] In 1840 John
Coppinger was granted a tract of land two and one-half by three-fourths
leagues in San Mateo County, which he called Cañada de Raymundo. Robert
Ridley received as a grant Rancho Collayomi in Sonoma County. John Read
operated a rancho two leagues east of Richardson's establishment at
Sausalito, on which he stocked 4,000 head of cattle.[59]

The Rancho Estero Americano has a most interesting history. According to one account, General Vallejo, commandant of the northern frontier,
in carrying out his orders to contain peacefully the Russians in their
settlement at Bodega, offered this rancho, which bordered on the alien
land, to James Dawson and Edward McIntosh. They agreed to develop the
property so as to preempt it from further Russian encroachment.[60] When
it came time to establish the claim officially, although the petition for
the title was made out in the name of the two partners and James Black, a
third Britisher, the grant was made only to "Eduardo M. Mackintosh". The
most probable reason for this procedure was that McIntosh was the only
one of the three who was a naturalized citizen of Mexico at the time.
When Dawson discovered that the grant was in McIntosh's name alone, he
was so outraged at this supposed duplicity that, after flogging McIntosh,
he sawed their house in two and moved his half to another rancho. This
tract of land, known as the Rancho Cañada de Pologome was later granted
to Dawson, and the title was confirmed to his widow, after the change of
flags, by the United States Land Commission.

James Black, besides having an interest in the Rancho Estero
Americano, was also granted a rancho of his own bordering on the Russian
settlement. It was listed as of two square leagues or more precisely
10,786.51 acres. Black was born in 1807 in Inverness, Scotland, and
after spending some time as a young man at sea, he was put ashore sick
at Monterey in 1832. Having recovered from his sickness, he hunted for
several years with Edward McIntosh before being settled by General
Vallejo on the Cañada de la Jonive rancho. During the Gold Rush Black
drove large herds of cattle to the mines each year, where he found a
ready market for them. Under American rule he held several minor political posts and died in 1870 at the age of 64.[61]

General Vallejo was also instrumental in aiding Timothy Murphy, an
Irishman by birth, for whom the General had acquired a personal liking.
He provisionally granted Don Timoteo generous acreage in San Rafael
County near his own property. The grant of Rancho San Pedro y Gallinos
to "Timeteo Morfil" was listed officially in Monterey on February 14, 1844.

---

58. Mofras, op. cit., I, 236.
59. Mofras, op. cit., I, 236.
60. History of Marin County, California, etc., (San Francisco,
1880), pp. 284-285.
61. Marin Co., pp. 284-285.

This land plus Rancho Santa Margarita, which Murphy also owned, embraced about five square leagues or 21,678.69 acres.

Sir George Simpson on his visit to Vallejo at Sonoma, camped for the night on Murphy's property. He makes the following entry in his journal:

The place of our encampment was once a part of the lands of the Mission of San Rafael, and now the property of an Irishman of the name of Murphy; and as we had started without a stock of provisions, we were glad to find ourselves the guests of a gentleman who besides our claim as fellow subjects, had got his cattle on so easy terms. Having made up our minds, therefore, to share with Mr. Murphy the spoils of the Church, we sent out several hunters to bring home a bullock for supper, but to our great mortification, we were less successful in plundering our host than he had been in plundering the priests; for our emmissaries had not been able to approach within shot of a single animal, a man on foot being such a prodigy in this land of laziness as to make the cattle scamper on in dismay.[62]

Vallejo was concerned over the poor quality of sheep in California. The Spanish wool growers did not care to invite overseas competition by sending their fine Merinos to the New World. As a result, Murphy was sent by his chief to England to purchase pure bred sheep for the improvement of the General's flocks. He also brought back blooded bulls and swine for the General and several dogs of various types for himself.[63]

Under Vallejo's tutelage Murphy was made major domo of the San Rafael Mission, which Vallejo regarded as part of his own province.[64] After the American conquest, Murphy made an unsuccessful claim for the Mission property on behalf of the San Rafael Indians.

Another English ranchero of note was Benjamin Foxen, who came to California in 1828 as a sailor on the ship Courier. He was baptized as Guillermo Domingo, married a native girl, and in 1837 was naturalized. On April 29, 1842 he was granted a rancho of two square leagues, called Tinaquaic, in Santa Barbara County, north of Gaviota Pass. Besides grazing cattle, Foxen farmed part of the land, raising corn, vegetables, and wheat -- getting seventy bushels per acre.[65]

In 1846 Foxen rendered a notable service to the United States

---

62.   Simpson, op. cit., I, 304.
63.   McKittrick, op. cit., p. 174.
64.   Ibid., p. 162. Vallejo successfully defied Hartnell,
Visitador General, to interfere in the management of the Mission.
65.   Bryant, op. cit., p. 410.

forces. In December of that year Fremont marched southward from Monterey to invest Los Angeles from the north as Stockton and Kearny approached from the south. He camped for a brief period near Tinaquaic before proceeding southward, and Foxen supplied the Americans with beef, flour, and horses. As Fremont was about to resume his march, which would take him through Gaviota Pass, Foxen found out from his native wife that the Californians were planning to ambush the invaders in that narrow defile. By rolling boulders down from the surrounding hills, they hoped to destroy at least part of the American force and perhaps trap the rest in the valley, where the foreigners could be picked off at leisure. Foxen warned Fremont of the plot and volunteered to guide him over San Marcos Pass by means of a little known path. It was this route that Fremont used successfully, although at great hardship and with the loss of many of his animals.[66]

The Californians regarded Foxen as a traitor, and after the conquest he was burned out of his home three times, and his cattle were stampeded and killed. Finally, he was forced to move away from this isolated spot. It was seven years before he dared to return to his rancho, where he lived for the rest of his life, dying in 1874.[67]

Hugo Reid, as a result of his marriage to the Indian woman, Dona Victoria, in 1837, could claim the ranchos Santa Anita and La Huerta del Cuati.[68] Dona Victoria had a vague title to both these pieces of land, which was later acknowledged by the provincial authorities. Santa Anita encompassed three square leagues, while La Huerta del Cuati was a small rancho of only 128.26 acres. Reid not only grazed cattle, but planted fruit trees, a vegetable garden, grape vines, and grain. William Heath Davis, a frequent visitor at Santa Anita, described it as "...the most picturesque spot of Southern California, with mountains, valley, springs, and running silvery streams."[69] In 1847, to acquire some ready cash, Reid sold Santa Anita to Henry Dalton, another Britisher, for $2,700 or twenty cents an acre. After Reid's death, Dona Victoria's claim to La Huerta del Cuati was rejected by the United States Land Commission.

One of the most important land holders in southern California was William Workman, who came overland in 1841 as co-leader of the Workman-Rowland Party. Born in England in 1800, Workman had emigrated to the United States, first settling in St. Louis and then in New Mexico. In

---

66. Mrs. Walter D. Benefield, "Benjamin Foxen's Great Service to United States," The Grizzly Bear, V. 47, 46-48.
67. Owen H. O'Neill, History of Santa Barbara County. State of California. Its People and Its Resources (Santa Barbara, Calif., 1939), pp. 132-133.
68. Dakin, op. cit., p. 51.
69. Ibid., p. 73.

1845 he was granted, in partnership with Rowland, the Rancho La Puente de San Gabriel, a tract of 48,790.55 acres in Los Angeles and San Bernardino Counties. Davis estimates their stock at 5,000 cattle, 500 horses, and 5,000 sheep.[70]

On June 8, 1846 Workman and Hugo Reid were sold, by order of Governor Pico, the Mission San Gabriel and the lands that had been left to it. The purchasers were to put up $7,000, pay the debts of the Mission, and support the padre.[71] There was evidence of fraud in this transaction, as well as in Pico's other sales of 1846, and it was ruled invalid by the United States District Court in 1855.

After he had divided the Rancho La Puente with his partner, Workman accumulated a fortune by devoting his energies to stock raising, cultivation of vineyards, and wine making.[72] In 1868 he entered the banking business in Los Angeles, but the bank failed in 1876, and Workman committed suicide.[73]

Through grants and purchases John Forster became one of the largest landholders in all of California. He was born in Liverpool, England in 1814. First coming to California at the age of 19, he continued to make numerous trips up and down the coast on the _Facio_, a ship belonging to his uncle, Santiago Johnson, another British pioneer in California. From 1840 to 1843 Forster was engaged as a shipping agent in San Pedro and a part of the time acted as Captain of the port.[74]

In 1837 he married Dona Ysador Pico, sister of Don Pio and Don Andres Pico, a fact which may account for the great amount of land which Forster accumulated. During his governorship Don Pio made many large grants and sold and leased several of the missions, principally to his friends and Britishers. "The kindest explanation of Don Pio's extensive land grants is probably the correct one. He saw the American invasion coming closer, and tried to save what he could for his friends and family. Of course he failed for very few of these hasty 'grants' were honored by the Americanos."[75]

On April 5, 1845 Forster was granted a tract of land known as Potreros de la Sierra Del Agua Caliente, near San Juan Capistrano. On December 11 of that same year he was granted Rancho Nacional, six square leagues in San Diego County. On this site the present cities of National City, Chula Vista, Bonita, and Lincoln are located. With James McKinley he purchased in 1846 Mission San Juan Capistrano for $710. The sale of

---

70. Davis, _op. cit._, p. 393.
71. Dakin, _op. cit._, p. 120.
72. _Los Angeles County_, p. 658.
73. Bancroft, _Calif._, V, 781.
74. _Los Angeles County_, pp. 470-471.
75. Dakin, _op. cit._, p. 131.

this mission, two others sold in 1845, and one sold in January, 1846, was approved by the United States Land Commission. He also bought up claims to other ranchos and after the conquest was successful claimant for Rancho Valle de San Felipe, embracing three square leagues in San Diego County; Trabuco, five square leagues in Los Angeles County, and Mission Vieja or La Paz, 46,432.65 acres in Los Angeles County.[76]

In 1844 Forster moved to San Juan Capistrano to look after his property interests. During the American conquest, he helped his brother-in-law, Pio Pico, to escape from Fremont's forces, which were seeking to capture him.[77] At a later time, when Stockton and Kearny were moving northward from San Diego toward Los Angeles in December, 1846, and January, 1847, Forster was a frequent visitor in the American camp. He kept Stockton informed of the movements of the Californians, led by another brother-in-law, Andres Pico, and aided the Commodore in obtaining supplies.[78]

After California became a part of the United States, Forster led the rest of his life as a peaceful _ranchero_ and died in 1882.[79]

Edward Stokes, an English sailor turned _ranchero_, came to California in 1840 on the _Fly_. He married Refugia, daughter of Jose Joaquin Ortega, and in 1845 with Ortega was grantee of the Rancho Valle de Palmo y Santa Isabel. In 1846 as Kearny's troops were approaching San Diego, they encamped near this rancho, and John S. Griffin, assistant surgeon, makes the following entry in his diary:

> Last night we had a visit from an Englishman, by name of Stokes, who owns a Ranch some fifteen miles distant, he has remained neutral during the difficulties, taking sides with neither party. I believe he was a sailor -- took a fancy for farming, at which he seems to have succeeded very well as he is represented as owning several Ranches and some thousand head of cattle...[80]

Another member of Kearny's forces gives us a more personal picture of Stokes.

----

76. Hoffman, _op. cit._, Index numbers 247, 437, 438, 491, 562.
77. Bancroft, _Calif._, V, 278.
78. John S. Griffin, _A Doctor Comes to California the Diary of John S. Griffin, Assistant Surgeon with Kearny's Dragoons, 1846-1847_ (San Francisco, 1943), p. 43.
79. Newmark, _op. cit._, p. 332, 531.
80. Griffin, _op. cit._, p. 92fn.

...he appeared in our camp, presenting a very singular and striking appearance. His dress was a black velvet English hunting coat, a pair of black velvet trousers, cut off at the knees and open on the outside of the hip, beneath which were drawers of spotless white; his leggins were of black buck-skin, and his heels armed with spurs six inches long. Above the whole bloomed the broad merry face of Mr. Stokes the Englishman.[81]

In spite of his professed neutrality, Stokes offered to carry a letter from Kearny to Stockton, then at San Diego.[82] This letter, delivered to Stockton on December 3, 1846, was the first direct communication between the two leaders. In it Kearny informed Stockton of his approach, asked for information on the state of affairs in California, and requested that a party be sent to open communications. Said he, "You might use the bearer, Mr. Stokes, as a guide to conduct your party to this place."[83] As a result, Captain Gillespie and a small group of men were despatched to rendezvous with Kearny.

On December 4th Kearny and his party proceeded from Warner's rancho to Stokes' Santa Isabel, where they were well received. "We found the buildings here much better than at Warners...Seignor Bill /Stokes' majordomo/ treated us with the most distinguished hospitality giving a supper to the officers -- turning out his mutton, grapes, and tortillas in great profusion. This was good, but his wine was abominable."[84] This episode must have been a pleasant respite after the ardors of the transcontinental journey and in preparation for the unfortunate battle of San Pascual. However, one writer has gone so far as to say that the American defeat was a result of the California wine.[85]

Unfortunately, despite Stokes' apparent prosperity, further records of his adventures are not available.

6. THREE IMPORTANT MEN IN EARLY CALIFORNIA -- RICHARDSON, FORBES, HARTNELL.

In order to illustrate the part played by men of British birth in

---

81. William H. Emory, Notes of a Military Reconnaissance, from Fort Beavenworth, in Missouri to San Diego, in California, quoted in Griffin, op. cit., p. 92fn.
82. Griffin, op. cit., p. 44.
83. Bancroft, Calif., V, 329.
84. Griffin, op. cit., p. 46.
85. Ibid., p. 93fn.

California, a more extended sketch will be given of the lives and activities of three of the most influential -- William A. Richardson, James Alexander Forbes, and William E. P. Hartnell.

William A. Richardson, mariner, merchant, land owner, founder of San Francisco, was one of the best known Englishmen in California. Born in Kent in 1795, he reached San Francisco Bay on August 2, 1822 as first mate of the British whaler Orion. There is some question as to whether he deserted or received a discharge from the ship's Captain.[86] At any rate on October 7, 1822 he petitioned Governor Sola for permission to remain.

> William A. Richardson, a native of Great Britain, and a resident of this Province, hereby respectfully represents: that he arrived at the port of San Francisco on the second day of August last, as mate of the British Whaleship Orion, and your Worship having approved of my staying here, and it being my intention to remain permanently and become domiciled in this Province at some place with suitable climate, I most humbly pray that your Worship be pleased to grant me this privilege and favor.
>
> William A. Richardson
> San Francisco, Presidio, Oct. 7, 1822

The governor placed the following endorsement on the margin of Richardson's petition:

> Monterey, October 12, 1822
>
> Being aware that the petitioner, besides being a navigator, is conversant with and engaged in the occupation of a carpenter, I hereby grant the privilege he asks for with the obligation that he shall receive and teach such young men as may be placed in his charge by my successor.
>
> Sola[87]

Richardson was baptized as Guillermo Antonio in 1823 and two years later married Maria Antonia Martinez, daughter of the commandant of the Presidio. According to Davis this romance had been blossoming since

---

86. Bancroft, Calif., II, 478. Thomas P. Burns, "The Oldest Street in San Francisco", California Historical Society Quarterly, xiii, 235, takes the position that he was discharged. Marguerite Eyer Wilbur in a footnote to Bryant, op. cit., p. 318, says that Richardson deserted.
87. Davis, op. cit., p. 8.

the day of Richardson's arrival. When he piloted a boat to the Presidio beach, he found there most of the inhabitants of that garrison, including Dona Maria, attracted by the anchoring of a foreign ship. As Richardson stepped ashore Dona Maria turned to her companions and said, "Oh, que hombre tan hermose el extranjero que desembarco del boto; el va hacer mi novio y yo voy hacer su esposa."[88]

In 1829 Richardson moved his family from San Francisco to San Gabriel, where he made his home for the next several years, although he sailed up and down the coast on various trading adventures. In May, 1835 Richardson met Governor Figueroa, who approved of his plan to establish a village at Yerba Buena and promised him a lot 100 varas square on the proposed site of the new settlement. Leaving San Gabriel that same month, Richardson and his family arrived in Yerba Buena on June 25, 1835. There he built, from posts and an old sail, the first habitation in what was to become the city of San Francisco. In October, having acquired legal possession of the lot for $25, Richardson built a three room wooden house, which in turn was superseded by a large adobe building in 1836. This property was sold to another Britisher, James McKinley, five years later when Richardson moved across the Bay.[89]

In 1835 Richardson was appointed Captain of the Port of San Francisco, a position which he occupied until 1844. Under American rule he was appointed Collector and Captain of the Port by Commodore Stockton. His duties were such that he was able to continue his private enterprises of shipbuilding, operating a ferry, and trading about the Bay. In 1841 he moved to Sausalito, a rancho fronting on the Bay, which had been granted to him in 1835, and began a profitable business selling fresh supplies to whaling ships.

Richardson died in 1856, leaving a widow and three children. He was "...a skillful sailor and an energetic man of business."[90] In addition, says Davis, "During Richardson's long life in California he made friends with all who came in contact with him in social or business relations."[91]

James Alexander Forbes was one of the most important pioneers of British birth, being a merchant and landowner, and serving from 1843 to 1847 as British vice-consul, the only official representative of Great Britain in California. William Heath Davis states that he was esteemed

---

88. "Oh, what a handsome man /is/ that foreigner just landed from the boat. He will be my bridegroom, and I will be his wife." Davis, op. cit., p. 10.
89. See Burns, "Oldest Street," loc. cit., xiii 235-239; "Yerba Buena Biographies: William A. Richardson", California Historical Society Quarterly, xiv, pp. 123-124; "Report on the First House in Yerba Buena", California Historical Society Quarterly, XI, 73-78; Soule, op. cit., p. 163; Dana, op. cit., p. 281.
90. Bancroft, Calif., V. 694.
91. Davis, op. cit., p. 12.

and respected by all who had social or business relations with him.[92]
Forbes was born in Inverness, Scotland, and according to one account, as
a young man accompanied his uncle, a British official, to Spain where he
was graduated from the College of Salamaca.[93] At any rate he was well
educated, a Spanish scholar speaking French and Spanish fluently.[94]

Forbes lived in South America for several years before coming to
San Francisco in 1830 or 1831. For a year or two he was employed as a
clerk by Padre Viader in Santa Clara, and then went into business for
himself. In 1834 he was naturalized and in that same year married Ana
Maria Galindo. The amalgamation that was taking place between the Anglo-
Saxon and Spanish cultures is indicated by the names of their twelve
children: Carlos, Martha, James Alexander, Jr., Michael, Frederick,
James Alonzo, Luis Felipe, Maria Clara, Juan Telesfore, Margaret, Francis,
and Alfred.[95]

After settling in San Jose, he was selected as a representative of
the Hudson's Bay Company in California. Said Mofras, "Forbes is an active
and energetic young man, and an ideal type to further the ambitions of
the company..."[96] He held the title of agent in 1836, elector in 1838,
and sindico in 1839. When Rae, manager of the Hudson's Bay Company's
post in San Francisco, committed suicide in 1845, Forbes was given the
job of looking after the company's interests there until the post could
be closed down.[97]

Besides his official duties and commercial interests, Forbes undertook the obligations of a landowner and _ranchero_. On August 21, 1839 he
was granted the Rancho San Pedro y San Pablo and on February 29, 1844
the Rancho Potrero de Santa Clara. Just before the Bear Flag Revolt he
acquired the Santa Clara Mission buildings[98] and was living there when
Chester Lyman, an ex-professor at Yale, visited him in 1847.[99]

In 1842 Forbes was appointed British vice-consul at Monterey but
did not undertake his official duties until the following year. His immediate superior was Eustice Barron, the British vice-consul at Tepic.

----

92. _Ibid._, p. 397.
93. Eugene T. Sawyer, _History of Santa Clara County with Biographical Sketches_, (Los Angeles Historic Record Co., 1922), p. 878.
94. Davis, _op. cit._, p. 346, 397.
95. _A Memorial and Biographical History of Northern California_,
(Chicago, 1891), p. 49.
96. Mofras, _op. cit._, I, 222.
97. Davis, _op. cit._, p. 93.
98. J. Alexander Forbes /Jr./, _The Golden West; Souvenir; Respect-
fully Dedicated to the Native Sons and Native Daughters of the State:
Primitive Years in California_ (n.p., 1919), p. 74.
99. Lyman, _op. cit._, p. 217.

Thomas Larkin, American consul in Monterey, reported to Washington that Forbes was a man of moderate wealth whose official position and private interests came into conflict, and who wished to see the United States take California.[100]

During the American conquest, he intervened as a private citizen, to bring the battle of Santa Clara to an end. After a brief skirmish between the Californians and the American forces on January 2, 1847, the former received word that their reenforcements from Monterey had been prevented from coming up by the action of the United States troops there. They therefore asked for a truce, and Forbes at the request of the American Commanding officer, Captain Marston, acted as intermediary at the conference. Forbes undertook this role, as he said, "...being convinced of the utter impossibility of their /the Californians'/ ultimate success, their want of everything necessary even for a brief resistance being quite palpable; and also being aware of the ruthless disposition of the volunteers who had another aim that to destroy the property and lives of the unfortunate Californians..."[101] An armistice was arranged, and the Californians were promised fair treatment.

After the conquest Forbes was involved in the New Almaden quick silver mines and the vast amount of litigation connected with them.[102] The claim of the British company was disallowed by the land commission and the American courts in what appeared to be sharp practice.[103] "In later years he led a life of retirement, nursing his intense, and perhaps not unfounded, bitterness against all that was American, and died at Oakland in '81, at the age of 77."[104]

William Edward Petty Hartnell was born in Lancashire, England in 1798. Little is known of his activities before reaching California in 1822, although it is known that he spent several years in South America prior to that time. In 1818 James Brotherston and Company of Liverpool, England, established a branch firm in Santiago, Chile under the name of John Begg and Company. The latter company extended its operations to other South American cities and finally reached up the Pacific coast to Monterey when McCulloch, Hartnell and Company became the first mercantile

---

100. Thomas O. Larkin to James Buchanan, June 1, 1846. William R. Manning, Diplomatic Correspondence of the United States. Inter-American Affairs. 1831-1860 (12 vols., Washington, D. C., 1936), VIII, 858-859.
101. E. A. Wiltsee, "The British Vice Consul in California and Events of 1846," California Historical Society Quarterly, X 125-126.
102. Sherman, op. cit., pp. 30-34.
103. John Walton Caughey, California (New York, 1940), p. 373.
104. Bancroft, Calif., III, 743.

house in California.[105]

Hartnell and Hugh McCulloch arrived in Monterey on board the John Begg in June, 1822. Their purpose was to obtain a contract to purchase hides and tallow from the missions, paying for them with cash or goods. Both Governor Sola and the prefect, Payeras, gave their consent, but each mission had the option of accepting or rejecting the contract, which was to last for three years. For the most part the missions were eager to take advantage of this trading opportunity. The contract, going into effect on January 1, 1823, was based on the following prices: hides, $1; wheat, $3 per fanega; tallow, $2 per arroba of 25 pounds; suet, $3; lard, $4; soap, $16 per 100 pounds; beef in pickle, including bone, $4 per hundred weight.[106] McCulloch and Hartnell, or "Macala and Arnel" as the house was known in California, obligated itself to send at least one ship each year to pick up the mission produce.

During the three years that the contract was in force, more than a dozen different McCulloch and Hartnell ships came to California, some of them making two, three, or more trips. Hartnell remained in Monterey to manage the California business while McCulloch returned to Chile. For a brief time this trading venture was quite successful but soon encountered insurmountable obstacles. In the first place the hide and tallow industry in California was completely unorganized at that time. Neither the merchants nor the natives knew the best way to prepare the hides for long shipment; collection points had to be established; ships arrived at the wrong time of year; the missions demanded specialized types of goods. All these and many other difficulties plagued McCulloch, Hartnell and Company. Secondly, other merchants soon appeared, buying up all the hides outside the contract, and causing discontent among the people within the contract. Thirdly, the company's market was dependent on the South American situation. As the wars of liberation ended, the market there for certain produce declined, and competition in the European market from South American products increased. In 1828 Hartnell, after taking on his own account the unsold goods, sailed for South America to dissolve the partnership.

In the meantime Hartnell was becoming a thorough-going Californian.[107]

---

105. The following account of this company's activities is taken from Adele Odgen, "Hides and Tallow: McCulloch, Hartnell and Company, 1822-1828", California Historical Society Quarterly, VI, 254-264.
106. Bancroft, Calif. Pastoral, p. 466.
107. In 1822 or 1823 he built the Hartnell adobe on the site now occupied by the Monterey Hospital. In 1851 this house was assessed to Hartnell at $2,700. M.S. WPA Historical Survey of the Monterey Peninsula. File 79. pp. 89-90.

He was baptized at San Carlos as Guillermo Eduardo in 1824, and the following year he married the young lady whom Alvardo describes as the "intelligent and beautiful Maria Teresa de la Guerra."[108] After being naturalized in 1830, he began the life of a ranchero at Alisal in partnership with the Soberanes, this step being dictated by his lack of success in commercial affairs.

It was not long before Hartnell was drawn into political affairs. In 1831 Governor Victoria's stern rule resulted in a successful revolution in the southern part of the province led by ex-Governor Echaendia. The foreign residents at Monterey had favored Victoria, in spite of his dictatorial acts, because he had been able to preserve order. Now they proceeded to organize a compania extranjero to defend Monterey and chose Hartnell as their leader.[109] The support of the compania extranjero was thrown behind Zamorano, who was eventually recognized as governor in the north while Echaendia contrived to hold the south. In 1833 a regularly appointed governor, Figueroa, relieved both men and once again united the province.

From 1833 to 1836 Hartnell acted as agent for the Russian-American Fur Company. His duties were to obtain cargoes of produce for the company and, if possible, to negotiate certain trading concessions for the Russians.[110]

Hartnell soon decided to augment his all too meager income by opening a school at the Rancho Alisal "...to educate young men for a business or professional life."[111] Besides being well educated, Hartnell had accumulated one of the few libraries in California. In addition, he was "the best linguist in the country", speaking French, Spanish, German, Italian, and being familiar with Hebrew, Russian, Greek and Latin.[112] In connection with Hartnell's school teaching days, it has been remarked that his own children frequently formed a majority of the pupils. This fact would not necessarily imply, however, that the school's roster was strictly limited for Hartnell's crowning glory was "...a circle of children, in which yours, my gentle reader, would only appear as a few more added to a sweeping flock..."[113] The generally accepted figures for Hartnell's family are twenty boys and five girls.[114]

---

108. Sanchez, op. cit., p. 139.
109. Bancroft, Calif., III, 220-223.
110. Ibid., IV, 162.
111. Robinson, op. cit., p. 195.
112. Sanchez, op. cit., p. 226; Colton, op. cit., p. 422.
113. Colton, op. cit., p. 422.
114. Lyman, op. cit., p. 225.

Hartnell's teaching experience was never a great success, and he accepted several government posts in order to provide for his large family -- at various times being _regidor_, collector of taxes and customs, official interpreter, and visitador general of the missions. Early in 1839 in an effort to repair some of the damage done by the inefficient management of the secularized missions, Governor Alvarado issued a new _reglamento_ for their administration. Hartnell was employed at a salary of $2,000 per year to carry out the _reglamento_. His duties were to make a tour of inspection, systematize the mission administration in a general way, and to hear complaints and to introduce minor reforms. He carried out his duties faithfully and well, but his powers were too restricted and the disintegration of the missions had been carried too far for any permanent good to be achieved.

After California was annexed by the United States, he served at various times as surveyor, appraiser of customs, and official interpreter and translator. In the last position he rendered valuable service in connection with legal matters and land claims and in the constitutional convention of 1849. Hartnell died in 1854 at the age of 56.

Bancroft appraises him as follows: "Hartnell was a man who enjoyed and merited the respect and friendship of all who knew him, being perfectly honest and straightforward in all his transactions, of most genial temperament, and too liberal for his own interests....He was not a good business manager, lacking application, method, and energy, and being always in financial trouble; but in any clerical or subordinate capacity he was most reliable and efficient."[115]

7. THE HUDSON'S BAY COMPANY IN CALIFORNIA

The Hudson's Bay Company was instrumental in bringing to California other British pioneers and for a brief period conducted various financial ventures in the province. The overland expansion of this company had finally brought it to the Pacific coast in the second decade of the nineteenth century, and its fur trappers were soon to penetrate into California. "...From Fort Vancouver on the Columbia, brigades of beaver trappers set out in all directions, and one of these, the Umpqua brigade, came regularly into the California hinterland, the Sacramento-San Joaquin Valley."[116] Professor Herbert E. Bolton in his forward to _Fur Brigade to the Bonaventura_ states that in the two decades following 1824, the Hudson's Bay Company probably took more beaver skins and other peltry from California than all the American fur trappers -- such as Ewing, Young, Smith, the Patties, J. J. Warner -- combined.[117] Mofras wrote that in 1830, Jean Baptiste Desportes MacKay, one of the company's hunters, took

---

115. Bancroft, _Calif._, III, 778.
116. Caughey, _op. cit._, p. 215.
117. John Work, _Fur Brigade to the Bonaventura: John Work's California Expedition 1832-1833 for the Hudson's Bay Co._ (San Francisco, 1945), p. iii.

more than 4,000 beaver skins in six months near Carquinez Bay.[118]

The California bound brigades made up of the hunters, their Indian wives, and their children, set out from Fort Vancouver in the fall.[119] Normally there was little contact with the permanent settlements on the coast, but what there was seemed to be cordial enough.[120] The following is a list of Hudson's Bay Company expeditions to California and their leaders:

1825	Finan McDonald and Thomas McKay
1826-1827	Peter Skene Ogden
1828-1829	Alexander Roderick McLeod
1830	Peter Skene Ogden
1832-1833	Michael Laframboise
1832-1833	John Work
1834	Michael Laframboise
1836	Thomas McKay, Stephen Meek, and Laframboise
1836-1837	Michael Laframboise
1839-1840	Michael Laframboise
1840-1841	Michael Laframboise and Thomas McKay
1842	Probably Laframboise
1843	Probably Ermatinger[121]

During this period the Hudson's Bay Company carried on a limited amount of trade by sea between Fort Vancouver and the settlements of California. Then in 1841 James Douglas, a representative of the Company, arrived in Monterey with the intention of establishing this trade on a permanent basis. After arranging for the continuance of the inland fur trapping expeditions and buying cattle to be driven overland to the Columbia, he conferred with Governor Alvarado concerning the establishment of a permanent post in California.[122]

When Douglas returned to Fort Vancouver, the plans and arrangements that he had made were approved by Dr. McLaughlin, the chief factor. As a result, William Glen Rae, McLaughlin's son-in-law, was sent in the company's ship Cowlitz to found the agency in California. Rae arrived in Monterey in August, 1841, and proceeded thence to San Francisco. At Yerba Buena he purchased for $4,500 a building and lot from Jacob Lesse, a prominent American-born merchant.[123] The property was bounded by Montgomery Street on the west, Sacramento on the south, Clay on the

---

118. Mofras, op. cit., I, 246.
119. Work, op. cit., p. iv.
120. Ibid., p. 37; Phelps, op. cit., p. 273.
121. Work, op. cit., p. v.
122. Herman Leader, "A Voyage from the Columbia to California in 1840 from the Journal of Sir James Douglas, "California Historical Society Quarterly, VIII, 98-107.
123. Davis, op. cit., pp. 91-92.

north, and the waters of the bay on the east. The building, a large, two-story, wooden structure, was used both as a store and a dwelling. Mrs. Rae arrived at the end of the year.[124]

The goods stocked by the agency were sent from England to the Hudson's Bay Company's post on the Columbia and were then reshipped to Yerba Buena.[125] There are conflicting reports on the success of the agency's business activities. Hittell in the History of San Francisco states that Rae was able to compete with other traders because of his policy of paying for hides and tallow in advance until 1844 when Sir George Simpson's disapproval forced him to discontinue this policy.[126] Captain Phelps gives a completely different version, indicating that the post failed because the company would not depart from its long established system of cash or barter, and no credit.[127] If it is true that Rae could not offer credit, he would be at a disadvantage because the Boston traders were willing to accept delayed payment.

William Heath Davis states that Rae was respected for his liberality and noted for setting a good table. "The captains, supercargoes, and other strangers were always welcomed at Rae's house, and it was a pleasure for him to entertain them. He had the true California nature and feeling in this respect."[128] He apparently also had the true California nature in regard to smuggling, for Davis lists him as one of the San Francisco merchants who bought up the excess stocks of whaling ships for their own private trade.

The activities of the Hudson's Bay Company in Yerba Buena were brought to a sudden and tragic close by Rae's suicide. On the morning of January 19, 1845, he blew out his brains in the presence of his wife. The motives for this act are somewhat obscure; "It is supposed, however, that his depression grew out of financial troubles, and his failure to manage the company's business successfully; and that it was aggravated also by the excessive use of intoxicating liquors."[129] There also may have been personal problems involved as Rae was reported to have been unfaithful to his wife and to have taken this way out when the rumor became public.[130] In addition, it is believed that Rae's depression was due in part to the failure of his political intrigues looking toward possible annexation of California to the British empire.[131]

---

124. Bancroft, op. cit., IV, 218.
125. Davis, op. cit., pp. 91-92.
126. John S. Hittell, A History of the City of San Francisco and Incidentally of the State of California (San Francisco, 1878), pp. 89-90.
127. Phelps, op. cit., p. 275.
128. Davis, op. cit., pp. 91-93.
129. Bancroft, Calif., IV, 593.
130. Davis, op. cit., pp. 91-94.
131. Caughey, op. cit., p. 216.

He was at the time involved in the revolt against Micheltorena, which gave all appearances of being a failure.[132]

Upon Rae's death, James Alexander Forbes took charge of the agency with instructions to close the business.[133] In the following year an agent, Mactavish, was sent down from Fort Vancouver to complete the liquidation of the property.[134] The land and the building were sold to Mellus and Howard, a business firm, for $5,000. The building was used first as a store, and then in the winter of 1849-1850 converted into the United States Hotel.[135]

8. GEOGRAPHICAL NAMES IN CALIFORNIA FROM BRITISH PIONEERS

A few British pioneers have had their presence in California commemorated by geographical features named in their honor. Most California names, however, are of Spanish and Indian origin on the one hand, or of Gold Rush vintage on the other.

First and foremost among the Englishmen comes Sir Francis Drake, after whom Drake's Bay has been named. It is a small indentation in the coast line, a few miles above San Francisco Bay, where Drake was supposed to have landed on his memorable visit to New Albion.

Among the more recent and more permanent British pioneers it is altogether fitting and proper that John Gilroy should have his name perpetuated by the city of Gilroy in northern California. He was the first foreigner to be permitted to remain in California, having been left sick with scurvy in Monterey by the Issac Todd in 1814. His real name was John Cameron, but having run away from home as a minor, he adopted the name of Gilroy to avoid being arrested and sent home.[136] In September, 1814, he was baptized at San Carlos as Juan Antonio Maria and in 1819 was granted permission to remain in California. Two years later he married Maria Clara de la Asuncion Ortega and was finally naturalized in 1833. In that same year the Ortegas obtained a grant of the Rancho San Ysidro, of which Gilroy was given one square league. On that site Gilroy built an abode house where he lived for the rest of his life. Beset by the sins of drinking and gambling he died in 1869 as poor as the day that he landed in California.[137]

---

132. Bancroft, Calif., IV, 494.
133. Davis, op. cit., pp. 91-94.
134. Larkin to Buchanan, April 17, 1846, Manning, Dip. Corres., VIII, 841-842.
135. Davis, op. cit., pp. 91-94.
136. Gilroy is said to have been his mother's maiden name. History of Santa Clara County, California, etc., (San Francisco, 1881), p. 274.
137. Bancroft, Calif., III, 757.

William A. Richardson has left his name to Richardson's Bay on the north side of San Francisco Bay between Marin Peninsula and Tiburon Peninsula. It was here that the whaling ships came for fuel, water, and fresh provisions. In the early days it was called Whalers' Bay or Whalers' Harbor.

In San Francisco Bay Blossom Rock, a shoal between Goat Island and Alcatraz Island, was named by Sir George Beechey for his ship H.M.S. Blossom. The rock was discovered and chartered by this expedition on its first visit to California.[138]

Another British explorer to become a big name in California was David Douglas, the naturalist. Douglas Park and the Douglas Fir serve as memorials to his brief visit to this province. He came to California in 1830 and spent two years collecting specimens and making scientific observations. Much to the amazement of the natives, he always did his exploring on foot, refusing the offer of horses and guides.[139] This was a fairly hazardous procedure because of the danger of bears and wild cattle. In 1834 in the Hawaiian Islands he was gored to death by a wild steer, having fallen into a pit trap into which the steer had previously blundered.[140]

In northern California the McCloud River, which originates in southern Siskiyou County and flows southward to join the Pit River, is named for Alexander McLeod, one of the Hudson's Bay Company's greatest trappers and expedition leaders.[141] He led at least one of the Umpqua brigades to the California back country.

The town of Inverness in Marin County was named in 1908 for the birthplace of James Black, a Scotch sailor and ranchero, who settled in this area about 1840.[142] Mill Valley, also in Marin County, takes its name from the saw mill built around 1843 by John Read on his rancho, Corte De Madera del Presidio.[143] Spence, a locality in northern Monterey County, situated within the boundaries of the Rancho Encinal y Buena Esperanza, is named for David Spence, the rancho's original owner.

Henry Dalton, a southern California ranchero, left his name to Rancho Azusa Dalton and to Big and Little Dalton Canyons in the Sierra Madre Mountains. Besides purchasing Rancho Santa Anita, Dalton acquired

138. Beechey, op. cit., p. 375.
139. Robinson, op. cit., p. 117; Davis, op. cit., pp. 206-207.
140. Robinson, op. cit., p. 118; Lyman, op. cit., pp. 123-124.
141. Phil Townsend Hanna, The Dictionary of California Land Names (Los Angeles, 1946), p. 162.
142. Hanna, op. cit., p. 133.
143. Ibid., p. 174.

part of the Rancho San Jose from the Palomares family as a gambling debt,[144] and part of Rancho Azusa, whose component parts became known as Azusa Dalton and Azusa Duarte.

The city of Livermore in Alameda County is named after Robert Livermore, an English sailor and _ranchero_, who came to California in 1822. He deserted from his ship, the _Conoliango_, as the _Colonel Young_ was known,[145] and spent several years working at various ranchos throughout the province. By 1837 he had established himself on the Las Pocitas rancho in what was later called Livermore Valley, and it was granted to him and Jose Noreiga on April 10, 1839. He later bought Don Jose out and also acquired the Rancho Canada de los Vacqueros, of three square leagues in Contra Costa. From his ranching and stock raising he became a wealthy man and maintained the reputation of an honest and hospitable citizen.[146]

Burney, Burrel, Clayton, Mt. Conness, Duncan Mills, and Thorton are also named for one time citizens of Great Britain, but who came to California after it became part of the United States.

9. BRITISHERS IN THE GRAHAM PARTY

In spite of the useful function that many Anglo-Saxons were serving, and their high position in the community, there were some foreigners who were not profitably employed, at least from the point of view of the native Californians. The result was that in 1840 nearly fifty Americans and Britishers were exiled in what has become known as the Graham party. In the late thirties an increasing number of the rougher type of foreigners -- trappers, traders, fronteirsmen -- entered California. these, in addition to a few unregenerated sailors, formed an unassimilated and dangerous element in the population.

Governor Alvarado, perhaps fearing a revolt in favor of independence or annexation to the United States, determined to rid the province of these undesirable men.[147] The immediate cause of his action was the

_____

144. Bess Adams Garner, _Windows in an Old Adobe,_ (Pomona, Calif., 1939), p. 56.
145. Bancroft, _Calif._, II, 478.
146. Bancroft, _Calif._, IV, 716; Bryant, _op. cit._, pp. 285-286.
147. The actual motives for Alvarado's action are hard to determine. Alfred Robinson in his _Life in California,_ p. 191, gives the following account: "Senor Alvarado firmly believed in the intention of Graham to revolutionize the country, although possessed of no facts to prove it. 'I was insulted,' he said, 'at every turn, by the drunken followers of Graham; and when walking in the garden they would come to its wall, and call upon me in terms of the greatest familiarity: 'Ho! Bautista, come here, I want to speak to you.' -- 'Bautista, here' -- 'Bautista, there' -- and Bautista

confession of one of the frontiersmen that an uprising had been planned under the leadership of Issac Graham. William R. Garner, an Englishman, was induced to offer more details of the proposed insurrection.[148] At any rate in the months of April and May, 1840, more than a hundred foreigners were seized, including some of the more substantial citizens.[149] The latter were soon released, as were most of those who had proper passports or who were married to native women. The remainder, some forty-six men, were shipped off to Tepic on their way to Mexico City to be dealt with by the Mexican authorities. Of this number twenty-three were British citizens, most of whom were undoubtedly ex-sailors.[150]

In Tepic the British vice-consul, Eustice Barron, immediately started proceedings to release the prisoners, and the British minister, Richard Pakenham, protested to the Mexican Foreign Minister stating that England would require action in behalf of the exiles.[151] Principally through the efforts of Barron, all of the men were released, although some of them were prohibited from returning to California. Of the others, those who desired it were given free passage back to California.

The seizure of the Graham men brought to California three foreign warships (one British), which came to protect the rights of their nationals. The French sloop-of-war _Danaide_ arrived in Monterey on June 11, 1840. When her Captain found that no Frenchmen had been deported, cordial relations were established, and the _Danaide_ remained for twenty days, enjoying the hospitality of the residents. On June 13, 1840 the United

---

147. Cont'd. from P. 74. - everywhere." Farnham, a violent partisan of the exiles, in his _Travels in California_, pp. 66-67, adds the following reasons: (1) Alvarado, when seeking Graham's support in the revolution of 1836 had promised him land and to raise him to power. Graham kept reminding the Governor of the promises which he wished to forget. (2) Alvarado and his supporters were heavily indebted to Graham as a result of some horse races. (3) The California girls preferred Americans and Britishers as husbands to their countrymen.
148. Garner was later reviled by the Graham men and their champion, Thomas Farnham, as one of the greatest villains of the piece. When Lyman reached Monterey in 1847, he found that Garner was suing Farnham for libel. Lyman, _op. cit._, p. 220.
149. Davis, _op. cit._, pp. 46-51.
150. The total number of exiles and of Englishmen within the group is controversial. Mofras, _op. cit._, I, 155, says 46 of which 25 were English. Bancroft, _Calif._, IV, 17, puts the number at 47. Chapman, _History of Calif._, p. 479, and Caughey, _op. cit._, p. 246, have put the number at 39. Richman, _op. cit._, pp. 475-476, gives the fullest account of Barron's work in Tepic, and I use his figures of 46 and 23.
151. Richman, _op. cit._, p. 476.

States man-of-war <u>St. Louis</u> reached the capitol, and her captain demanded an explanation, which, when given, was apparently satisfactory, for he took no action other than to collect testimony from a few of the residents. In November, after the furor had subsided, the English man-of-war <u>Curacoa</u> arrived in Monterey and prompted the final settlement of English claims.[152]

152. Bancroft, <u>Calif</u>., IV, 35-38.

CHAPTER IV

BRITISH DESIGNS ON CALIFORNIA

1   THE MEXICAN DEBT TO BRITISH BONDHOLDERS

A great deal has been written about England's attempts, in the period just before the American conquest, to add California to her colonial empire. England was supposed to have been active, especially in the decade before 1846, in promoting schemes to colonize California or to establish a protectorate over it. The fact that writers, contemporary with this period, and early historians were without accurate information led to many exaggerations and misconceptions. The truth of the matter can be summed up in the following brief statements: (1) Several prominent California leaders favored an English protectorate -- principally to forestall American annexation or to further their own personal ambitions. (2) English agents in California and other parts of the New World were anxious to acquire this territory. (3) The policy of the English government, on the other hand, if not actually hostile to such plans, was definitely cool toward them. (4) American leaders and the American people were apprehensive of British seizure of California.

Most of the plans proposed by British agents for the acquisition of California were connected with Mexico's debt to British bondholders. In order to understand these proposals it is necessary to trace the origin of the debt and the peculiar arrangements made for its retirement.[1]

Two loans to Mexico were made in London in October, 1823, and February, 1825, amounting to $32,000,000. Interest on these loans was paid until 1827 and then defaulted. In 1830 the Mexican Congress agreed to capitalize the past due interest up to April, 1831, and, in addition, half of the interest falling due up until 1836. This plan, which added seven and one-half million dollars to the debt, was approved by the British bondholders. Under the new arrangement interest was paid until July, 1832, and then again defaulted.

A conversion scheme was drawn up in 1837 and finally accepted by the Mexican administration and the creditors. New bonds were to be issued for one-half of the outstanding debt. The other half was to be covered by "deferred" bonds, on which no interest was to be paid until October 1, 1847. These "deferred" bonds might be exchanged at the holders

---

1. A clear and concise history of the debt and the plans for the acquisition of California based on it is given in Lester G. Engelson, "Proposals for the Colonization of California by England in Connection with the Mexican Debt to British Bondholders 1837-1846", California Historical Society _Quarterly_, XVIII (June 1939), 136-148.

option for warrants on vacant lands in Mexico at the rate of four acres for one pound sterling. The bonds not exchanged were to become interest bearing in 1847. The Mexican government agreed to hypothecate 100,000,000 acres of land in Texas, Chihuahua, New Mexico, Sonora, and California. At the bondholders request another 25,000,000 acres was hypothecated "...in a region suitable for colonization with the nearest communication to the Atlantic Ocean."[2]

The London agents of the bondholders, anticipating approval of the plan by Mexico, began to effect the conversion. The Mexican government delayed temporarily, but the plan was finally approved on June 1, 1839, at which time the debt exceeded $46,000,000. Of this amount one-third had already been converted. Interest on the first half of the debt remained unpaid and kept accumulating, but after more delays and misunderstandings, the Mexican government on December 13, 1843, recognized the debt as standing at $54,573,730.

In 1845 the Mexican Congress, acknowledging the failure of the colonization scheme, inasmuch as the deferred bonds, were not being exchanged for land warrants, endeavored to meet the difficulties that would arise in 1847 over the interest of these bonds. A law was passed providing that no further interest was to be capitalized, the interest rates were not to be raised, nor was the amount of the debt to be increased, nor was any national property to be alienated or hypothecated. While attempts were being made to convert the debt on this basis, war between the United States and Mexico intervened.

Says the foremost authority on the debt question:

The colonization proposal of 1837 was primarily designed to reduce the foreign debt by one-half and to secure occupation of vacant lands. The selection of the northern departments from Texas to California was evidently motivated by a desire to secure British assistance, through bondholding colonists, in protecting her northern frontier from "ambitious designs" by her neighbor on the north. Since most of the bondholders

_____

2. Texas, having proclaimed its independence, was incensed at the allocation of lands within her borders, and, of course, refused to accept responsibility for any of Mexico's public debt. However, she did offer to assume 1,000,000 pounds of the debt if Great Britain could induce Mexico to accept a truce with Texas. The bondholders indicated their willingness to accept land between the Nueces and Rio Grande Rivers instead of the money. (This proposal came to naught as Mexico refused to recognize Texas.) George B. Garrison, Diplomatic Correspondence of the Republic of Texas, Pt. III, Annual Report of the American Historical Association, 1908, vol. II, 909-910, 917-919.

were more interested in receiving cash than vacant land, the many negotiations on the debt and political developments in Texas, the region most desired, aided in defeating Mexico's attempt to preserve her northern departments.

There were, however, several sincere proposals for taking advantage of the "deferred" bonds, especially for the colonization of California. It was only natural that the press of jealous nations should interpret Her Majesty's financial support of the bondholders and known proposals for British colonization, or for the outright cession of California in payment of the debt, as bona fide evidence of British designs.[3]

2. SCHEMES TO COLONIZE OR TO ESTABLISH A PROTECTORATE OVER CALIFORNIA

The earliest scheme for exchanging the bonds for land in California was made by Alexander Forbes in his book, California: A History of Upper and Lower California, etc. Published in London in 1839, this was the first book in English relating wholly to California. Alexander Forbes, not to be confused with James Alexander Forbes, the British vice-consul in California, was a merchant in Tepic. He was a partner of Eustice Barron, the British vice-consul there, who had been instrumental in securing the release of the Graham party exiles, and who was to be involved in future schemes for English acquisition of California. Alexander Forbes had never been to California, but he had talked to merchants and sea captains who had.

Although ostensibly writing a history of California, Forbes was more concerned with exciting interest in its colonization. Said he, "Taking every circumstance into account perhaps no country whatever can excel or hardly vie with California in natural advantages."[4] The book contained chapters on California's topography, commerce, agriculture, and one on "Upper California considered as a Field and Foreign Colonization." After outlining California's trade with South America and the Pacific Islands, Forbes continues,

The foregoing is a brief view of what commercial consequences California might soon arrive at, if peopled by an active and enterprising race of men; but under the present system, and while the population retain their present character of indolence and total want of enterprise, it must stand still. If,

---

3. Engelson, loc. cit., XVIII, p. 138.
4. Alexander Forbes, California: A History of Upper and Lower California from their Discovery to the Present Time; Comprising an Account of the Climate, Soil, Natural Productions, Agriculture, Commerce, etc., (San Francisco, 1937), p. 195.

on the contrary, this country was under an enlightened and
liberal government, which knew how to promote its colonization,
and to encourage the resort of industrious settlers from whatever quarter they might come, it would not fail to become known
and selected as a refuge by the innumerable starving population
of the Old World; and would soon be one of the most interesting
and prosperous spots on the earth. It is true that its distance
from Europe is great, but it is not much greater than that to
New Holland or Van Dieman's Land, which so many emigrants now
reach at a moderate expense.[5]

Forbes offers two solutions to the expense of the trip from Europe.
He suggested that emigrants could be brought out in empty, outbound
whaleships sailing for the Pacific fisheries. His second solution was
to construct an isthmian canal.

Not only does he emphasize the desirability of taking California
and the ease with which it could be done, but he plays upon English
fears that another nation might move first.

The British government seems lately to have had some suspicion
that California would be encroached upon, if not taken entire
possession of, by the Russians who are settled so close upon
its northern frontier; but by the latest accounts no encroachment has been made, nor has any augmentation been made either
in the number of people in the colony, or in the fortifications.
The danger does not lie there. There is another restless and
enterprising neighbor from whom they will most probably soon
have to defend themselves, or rather to submit to: for although
the frontiers of North America are much more distant than the
Russian, yet to such men as the Back-settlers, distance is of
little moment, and they are already well acquainted with the
route. The northern American tide of population must roll on
southward, and overwhelm not only California, but other more
important states.[6]

Forbes' plan was to transfer California to England in return for
a cancellation of the Mexican debt. The province would be controlled
by the bondholders organized in a manner similar to the East India
Company.

If California was ceded for the English Debt, the creditors
might be formed into a company with the difference that they
should have a sort of sovereignty over the territory, some-

---

5. Forbes, op. cit., p. 195.
6. Forbes, op. cit., pp. 91-92.

what in the manner of the East India Company. This in my
opinion would certainly bring a revenue in time which
might be equal to the interest of the debt, and under good
management and with an English population, would most certainly realize all that has been predicted of this fine
country.[7]

This proposal was, of course, a purely private one and had no relation to Great Britain's foreign policy toward Mexico. Professor E. D.
Adams, from an investigation of diplomatic correspondence in the British
Record Office, has shown that the Foreign Office's first official
interest in California was a result of the Graham affair in 1840.[8] At
that time Barron was concerned because there was no British warship on
hand to be dispatched to Monterey. He was forced to appeal to the captain
of the United States corvette "San Luis" to investigate the claims of the
British exiles.[9] Both Barron and Pakenham were chagrined by the necessity
to ask for aid from the United States, and they urged an increase of naval
strength in the Pacific.[10]

From a question of naval prestige, Pakenham's interest in California
soon grew to one of colonization as a result of a conversation with
James A. Forbes, communications from Barron on the value of California,
and suspicions of French designs on that province, aroused by de Mofras'
activities. Pakenham formulated his own scheme of British colonization.
It too was based on the acquisition of land through the cancellation of
the Mexican debt. Said he,

> ...as relates to Texas, the arrangement must, of course, be
> considered a dead letter; and in the present circumstances
> of the Country, Chihuahua, and New Mexico are not eligible
> districts for colonization: but I believe there is no part
> of the World offering greater natural advantages for the
> establishment of an English colony than the Provinces of
> Upper California; while its commanding position on the
> Pacific, its fine harbours, its forests of excellent timber
> for ship-building as well as for every other purpose, appear
> to me to render it by all means desirable, in a political
> point of view, that California, once ceasing to belong to
> Mexico, should not fall into the hands of any Power but England;

---

7. Ibid., p. 93.
8. Ephraim Douglas Adams, British Interests and Activities in
Texas 1838-1846 and Addendum "English Interest in the Annexation of
California." (Baltimore, 1910), p. 236.
9. Refer to page 75 for an account of the arrival of United States
and British war vessels at Monterey as a result of the Graham affair.
10. Adams, op. cit., p. 130.

and the present debilitated condition of Mexico, and the gradual increase of foreign population in California render it probable that its separation from Mexico will be effected at no distant period; in fact, there is some reason to believe that daring and adventurous speculators in the United States have already turned their thoughts in that direction.[11]

Pakenham then gave details showing that it would not be difficult to form a company in England "....for the establishment of an English colony in California." Such a colony would at first be under Mexican soverignty, but "....this state of things would not last forever...."[12]

Pakenham's plan was the first one concerning California to be submitted to the Foreign Office, but although he was the British minister to Mexico, his project did not represent English governmental opinion. In fact it was directly opposed to the official attitude toward Mexico, the two countries were on friendly terms, and England was trying to strengthen Mexico so that she could resist the encroachments of the United States in Texas.[13]

Lord Aberdeen, the Foreign Secretary, submitted Pakenham's plan to the Colonial Office for consideration. Stanley's reply was forwarded back to the minister in Mexico without comment, indicating the Foreign Office's concurrence in its contents. This reply is a perfect statement of England's official policy toward California in particular, and all new colonies in general, during this period.

His Lordship directs me in answer, to acquaint you for the information of the Earl of Aberdeen, that he is not anxious for the formation of new and distant Colonies, all of which involve heavy direct and still heavier indirect expenditure, besides multiplying the liabilities of misunderstanding and collisions with Foreign Powers. Still less is Lord Stanley prepared to recommend the adoption of a plan whereby the Soil shall, in the first instance, be vested in a Company of Adventurers, with more or less of the powers of Sovereignty and of Legislation, and the Settlement so formed be afterwards placed under the protection of the British Crown; which as it seems to his Lordship is the position contended for by Mr. Pakenham.[14]

When Pakenham received this despatch, he lost all interest in California, neglecting even to appoint a vice-consul in Monterey, although

---

11. _Ibid._, p. 238.
12. Adams, _op. cit._, p. 238.
13. _Ibid._, p. 239.
14. Adams, _op. cit._, p. 240.

he had been granted permission to do so by a despatch dated February 26, 1841.[15]

The next British imperialist to write about California was Sir George Simpson. In his book describing his trip around the world, Simpson advocated taking California in exchange for part of the debt.[16] Later, however, in a letter from Honolulu, dated March 10, 1842, to Sir John H. Pelly, Governor of the Hudson's Bay Company, he proposed a different course.[17] In this letter, apparently intended for the eyes of the government, he outlined the advantages of California's soil, climate, geographical position, and fine harbor. He stated that British residents at one time hoped that California would fall into England's hands in liquidation of the Mexican debt, but now they felt that it would be a waste of money inasmuch as California could be acquired without this outlay. He wrote that the people of California wished to separate from Mexico, but they were apprehensive lest they would then be taken by the United States. It would require little encouragement to persuade them to declare their independence and place themselves under the protection of Great Britain. "Indeed it has been communicated to me, confidentially, and I feel authorized to say, that the presence of a British cruiser on the coast, with a private assurance of protection from Great Britain, and appointments given to the present higher authorities and officials which would not involve a larger sum than a few thousand pounds per annum, would be a sufficient inducement to declare themselves independent of Mexico and claim the protection of Great Britain."[18] This letter was delivered by Pelly to the Foreign Office, but it was later returned to him without comment.[19]

Soon thereafter another proposal was brought forward for the settlement of the debt in question, this one sponsored by President Tyler and Secretary of State Webster of the United States. In 1842 and 1843 a settlement, known as the "Tripartite Agreement", was urged by the United States as a means of clearing up the outstanding points of dispute between that nation, England, and Mexico. Its chief provisions called for a recognition of Texan independence by Mexico, the establishment of the Oregon boundary line at the Columbia, the cession of California to the United States, and the payment of several million dollars by the United States to Mexico, part of which would cover American claims and the remainder was to go to English creditors and bondholders. The plan was unsuccessful because of Mexican aversion to the alienation of national territory and because of Commodore James' premature seizure of Monterey.[20]

---

15. Ibid.
16. Simpson, op. cit., I, 327-238, 408-410.
17. Joseph Schaffer, "Letters of Sir George Simpson, 1841-1843", American Historical Review, XIV (October, 1908), 70-94.
18. Schaffer, "Letters," loc. cit., XIV, 89.
19. Ibid., XIV, 86.
20. Engelson, "Proposal," loc. cit., XVIII, 141-142.

Besides ending any hopes for the success of the Tripartite Agreement, Jones' action had the effect of bestirring Pakenham to appoint finally a vice-consul for California. James Alexander Forbes' appointment was dated December, 1842, but he did not undertake any official duties until October, 1843. In Forbes' early dispatches he indicated, as did his immediate superior, Barron, that Great Britain could secure California with very little effort.

With the passage of time, as hope for the redemption of the bonds faded away, the bondholders became more willing to speculate on the acceptance of Mexican lands. Most of them were interested in a site on the Gulf of Mexico in the vicinity of Texas. However, a few looked toward California, and of these Robert C. Wyllie was probably the most active. In 1843 he set about gathering material for a report on California, consulting Alexander Forbes and writing to William E. Hartnell for specific information.

Wyllie also despatched a long letter to Bocanegra, the Mexican Minister of Foreign Affairs, urging the colonization of Mexico's vacant land. He advocated a liberal land policy to encourage European immigration, and the proceeds from the sale of land could be applied against the debt to English bondholders. Wyllie further stated that the reason deferred bonds had not been exchanged for land warrants was that the Mexican government had neglected to issue the necessary decrees to implement such an exchange. (Wyllie himself had tried to convert 10,000 pounds in deferred bonds into the equivalent land warrants but had found the Mexican official uninstructed on this procedure.) If European colonists were encouraged to immigrate, he continued, they would become good citizens of Mexico, and at the same time protect the northern frontier from aggression.[21]

These letters, as well as an account of his attempts to get action from the Mexican officials, were published by Wyllie in his report to the bondholders.

Under date of April 20, 1844, Hartnell replied to Wyllie answering the questions that the letter had propounded. Information was supplied on freight rates, the amount of money in circulation, the whaling industry off the coast, seals and otters, the Hudson's Bay Company's establishment at Yerba Buena, rivers, doctors, missions, mines, customs duties, and other pertinent topics.[22] Hartnell also reported that his proposal for obtaining land for colonization had met with a favorable reception from Governor Micheltorena. Said he,

---

21. Engleson, "Proposals," loc. cit., XVIII, 143.
22. Lauro de Rojas, "California in 1844 as Hartnell Saw It", California Historical Society Quarterly, XVII (March, 1938), 25-26.

With respect to the latter part of your letter, I have spoken
to the Governor; no instructions whatever have been received
in Calif. touching the exchange of deferred bonds for lands.
But his Excellency had assured me that he will do all that he
possibly can for you with respect to granting a tract of land
for colonization his faculties do not allow him to give more
than 11 square leagues to one person, but I can ask for one
tract for you and another for myself, and I am almost certain
that I shall succeed in obtaining the privilege to hold on to
them a reasonably sufficient time to enable Settlers to come
out from England (say two years from the time they are
granted) without being obliged to stock or cultivate them
within one twelvemonth, as all others who have been obliged
to do. The Governor told me plainly that he wished very
much that Settlers would come out from Europe so that all the
vacant lands should not be given to Americans, and he even
hinted that he should like to take a share in the speculation
himself, he has always professed himself particularly favorable to the English.[23]

Wyllie replied to Hartnell in November, 1844, stating that only
Great Britain could save California from the United States. He urged
the Californian to get all the land he could if a crisis threatened and
indicated that, if Micheltorena wanted to favor their scheme, he could
have one-third of their share. After this letter nothing further was
heard of the Wyllie plan.

The first proposal to receive any official recognition, after
Pakenham's plan had been squelched by the Colonial Office, was originated by James A. Forbes, the new British vice-consul in California.[24]
It should be noted that this was one of the few intrigues that was not
related to the debt question and that it was concerned with the establishment of a protectorate rather than a colony.

On September 5, 1844, Forbes reported to Barron an interview with
a body of influential native Californians. They stated that they planned
to revolt against the Mexican government and wished to know if California
would be received under the protection of Great Britain. He forwarded this
proposition with the following statement:

I feel myself in duty bound to use all my influence to prevent
this fine country from falling into the hands of any other
foreign power than that of England. I repeat that it is impossible for Mexico to hold California for a much longer period,

---

23. de Rojas, "Hartnell", loc. cit., XVII, 26.
24. The following account of this proposal is taken from Adams,
op. cit., pp. 241-251.

and if the Govt. of Great Britain can with honor to itself, and without giving umbrage to Mexico, extend its protection to California, reaping those benefits which by proper management, would infallibly attend that protection, I should presume that it would be impolitic to allow any other nation to avail itself of the present critical situation of California for obtaining a footing in this country.[25]

Barron in turn despatched it to London on October 12, 1844, where it was received on December 13, 1844. The significance of this suggestion was that it was received by the Foreign Office at a time when Aberdeen had temporarily changed his policy toward Mexico because she refused to recognize the independence of Texas and because he had been informed that the United States would not be deterred from going into Texas by the threat of war. Aberdeen's reply, dated December 31, 1844, contained the "...most definite instructions upon California emanating from the British foreign office throughout the entire period."[26] But even as such it was most innocuous.

The present position of California is evidently very critical; and it appears to be pretty clear that unless the Mexican Government bestir themselves, an outbreak will in no long time take place in that Province, which may end in its separation from Mexico. Her Majesty's Government can have nothing to do with any insurrectionary movement which may occur in California; nor do they desire that their agents in that part of the world should encourage such movement. They desire, on the contrary, that their agents should remain entirely passive.

While California continues subject to Mexico it would be obviously contrary to good faith on the part of England to encourage a spirit of resistance or disobediance in the inhabitants of the Province against their Mexican rulers. It is therefore entirely out of the question that Her Majesty's Government should give any countenance to the notion which seems to have been agitated of Great Britain being invited to take California under her protection.

Her Majesty's Government do not pretend to determine as to the propriety of any step which may be taken by the inhabitants of California towards establishing their independence. In such matters no foreign nation has any right to interfere, except it be bound to such interference by Treaty with the Mother country;

---

25. Adams, op. cit., p. 243.
26. Ibid., p. 246.

which is not the case with Great Britain. It is, however, of importance to Great Britain, while declining to interfere herself, that California, if it should throw off the Mexican yoke, should not assume any other which might prove inimical to British interests. It will therefore be highly desirable that at the same time that it is intimated to the persons of authority in California that the relations which exist between Great Britain and Mexico prevent us from taking part in any proceedings of the Californians which may have for their object the separation of that province from Mexico, those persons should be clearly made to understand that Great Britain would view with much dissatisfaction the establishment of a protectoral power over California by any other foreign state.[27]

As it turned out this was not Great Britain's permanent policy because Mexico submitted to her desires, and the earlier friendly relations were resumed. Aberdeen, as a man of honor, was unwilling to authorize any British agent to stir up a revolutionary movement in California. However, he was not unwilling to accept the fruits of that revolution if they should fall into the hands of Great Britain.[28]

In the meantime Barron and Forbes continued to believe that Great Britain could easily acquire a protectorate over California, but when Aberdeen's despatch was received, they had to abandon their plans, realizing that the passive policy laid down would not achieve their ends. They, therefore, transferred their support to continued Mexican control, believing that it would be more beneficial for English interests than would independence. British agents in California remained inactive, and it was not until Fremont's arrival in the winter of 1845-1846 that Forbes was again stirred to action.[29]

The next plan for British colonization was made by an Irish priest, Eugene MacNamara.[30] His objectives were three-fold: "...to advance the cause of Catholicism..., to contribute to the happiness of my countrymen..., to put an obstacle in the way of further usurpations on the part of an irreligious and anti-catholic nation."[31] He proposed to bring over one thousand Irish families and establish colonies in the vicinity of San Francisco Bay, Monterey, and Santa Barbara. Each family was to receive a square league of land. MacNamara asked for a temporary exemption from taxation for the colonists, hypothecation of the land grants to pay for their transportation, and a gift of the customs duties at San Francisco for a period of several years. The

---

27. Adams, op. cit., pp. 247-249.
28. Ibid., 250.
29. Ibid., 251.
30. For an account of this plan see Bancroft, Calif., V, 215-223.
31. Ibid., V, 215.

priest presented his plan to the president of Mexico with the following admonition: "If the means which I propose be not speedily adopted, your Excellency may be assured that before another year the Californians will form a part of the American nation. Their catholic institutions will become the prey of methodist wolves; and the whole country will be inundated with these cruel invaders."[32]

A copy of MacNamara's plan was forwarded to Aberdeen by Bankhead, the British minister in Mexico, but it was not answered nor even acknowledged.

MacNamara received some encouragement in Mexico but was advised to go to California, select suitable lands, and submit his plan to the departmental authorities. He took passage on the HMS _Juno_ and arrived in Monterey at the end of May or in the first part of June, 1846.[33]

With some modifications MacNamara's plan was approved by the California assembly on July 7, 1846, and provision was made for the grant of three thousand square leagues of land -- the priest was now to bring three thousand Irish families -- between the San Joaquin River and the Sierra Nevada Range. Governor Pico signed the grant, apparently dating it back a few days to July 4, 1846, so as to antedate the raising of the United States flag on July 7th. The grant was also illegal in other respects, however, and Larkin told MacNamara that it would not be recognized by the United States. MacNamara returned to Mexico, and no attempt was made to secure recognition of the title in California.

Before leaving, the Irishman told Larkin that he was the agent of a private company in London. It is possible that this company was connected with the English bondholders, and that an attempt was being made to secure as much land as possible, foreseeing an increase in land values after the American conquest.[34]

The next colonization project was one by Mackintosh, a British consul in Mexico, to bring in 500,000 European immigrants in twenty years.[35] This scheme worked out in considerable detail followed the main outlines of the Pakenham plan. Apparently Mexican support was received for Paredas promised to give "every possible facility" in carrying out the proposal. Mackintosh sent his plan to Bankhead, who forwarded it on to Aberdeen. No reply was received by Bankhead or the promoters, Mackintosh and his London partners.[36] However, Aberdeen did speak of it to Thomas Murphy, the Mexican minister in London, observing

---

32. _Ibid._, V, 215-216.
33. Larkin to Buchanan, June 18, 1846, Manning, _Dip. Corres._, VIII, 866.
34. Engelson, Proposals," _loc. cit._, XVIII, 144.
35. Justin H. Smith, _The War With Mexico_ (2 vols., New York, 1919), I, 524; Engelson, "Proposals," _loc. cit._, XVIII, 145.
36. Engelson, "Proposals," _loc. cit._, XVIII, p. 145.

that it was too late to put the plan into action, that it would give offense to the United States as an obvious attempt to block its designs, and probably would be ineffective in competing with American immigration.[37]

As war between Mexico and the United States approached, Thomas Murphy, in a last effort to arouse English in California, obtained the assistance of Mr. Price, a partner of Mackintosh, and J. D. Powles, vice-chairman of the Mexican bondholders committee, in drawing up a new plan. A company was to be formed to buy up 50,000,000 pounds in deferred bonds and 1,250,000 pounds in cash. However, no support was forthcoming from the English government, and the idea was abandoned.[38]

In addition to the proposals for English colonization of California or for an English protectorate, there were recurrent rumors that England was going to buy California outright. Up until 1846 these rumors were entirely groundless as was shown by the offer when it was finally made. When war with the United States became inevitable, Paredes, the Mexican president, realizing that California would be lost anyway, offered to transfer it to England as security for a loan. Bankhead transmitted the offer to the Foreign Office with the statement, "It is an indirect offer of sale, and it is the first time that any such offer has ever been hinted at from a responsible authority."[39] Palmerston, who had resumed the position of Foreign Secretary, drafted the reply in complete consistency with his predecessor's policy, stating that England would not be interested in a treaty leading to the acquisition of California especially since Mexico, in the light of recent events, probably would not be able to carry out her end of the bargain, having lost her control of that province.[40]

Besides examining the English diplomatic correspondence, Professor Adams has investigated the instructions sent to British naval commanders in the Pacific, looking for evidence of a plot to seize California.[41] He concludes, "An examination of the letters to and from British admirals stationed on or near the Pacific Coast wholly negatives this suspicion and serves merely to emphasize the British government's lack of interest in California."[42]

In the period from 1841 to 1842 the correspondence of Admiral Thomas, commanding the British fleet in the eastern Pacific, was almost entirely about the French at Tahiti. The complete absence of any reference to California indicates that Commodore Jones' statement that he took Monterey to prevent British naval aggression was unfounded.

---

37. Sir Arthur Gordon, The Earl of Aberdeen (London, 1893), p. 183; Antonio de la Pena y Reyes, Lord Aberdeen, Texas y California (Mexico, 1925), pp. 43-44; Smith, op. cit., I, 302.
38. Engelson, "Proposals", loc. cit., XVIII, 145-146.
39. Adams, op. cit., p. 264.
40. Ibid., p. 263.
41. Ibid., pp. 253-261.
42. Ibid., p. 254.

Admiral Seymour, who was in command in 1844, was still primarily concerned with the Pacific Islands. Gradually he became more interested in California as a result of correspondence with Barron at Tepic, but his instructions were to watch the French, and it was often necessary for him to leave the coast for this purpose. Finally in March, 1846, he wrote to the Admiralty requesting an increase in naval strength in the Pacific, basing his request on the belief that war with the United States was possible. His objectives were to defend Oregon, "...to observe the proceedings of the United States relative to California," to protect Britain commerce, and to attack American commerce. Seymour's request was rejected by the Foreign Secretary on the grounds that war was not expected.

On May 11, 1846, soon after sending his request for an increase in strength, and before a reply was received, Seymour ordered the *Juno* to Monterey to protect British subjects and to observe events there. It was on this voyage that MacNamara journeyed to California. In accordance with Aberdeen's "passive policy" despatch of December 31, 1844 (a copy of which Seymour received late in 1845), Captain Blake of the *Juno* was instructed to use his influence in case the Californians announced their independence, to prevent them from accepting the protection of any other nation. Blake first stopped at Monterey but sailed, on June 17, 1846, for Santa Barbara where conferences were held with Vice-Consul Forbes and Governor Pio Pico, the leader of the pro-English party.[43] Both reported, however, that they simply advised Pico not to accept a protectorate from any foreign nation should California become free.[44]

In the meantime Seymour received information that the people of California were about to hold a convention at Santa Barbara with the intention of separating from Mexico and seeking the protection of some foreign power.[45] According to his information, this movement had

---

43. Larkin to Buchanan, June 18, 1846, Manning, Dip. Corres., VIII, 866.

44. Adams, op. cit., pp. 256-257.

45. A military junta had assembled in Monterey on April 2, 1846, to investigate means of protecting the province from foreign, i.e. American, aggression. It was reported that the junta also discussed the desirability of separating from Mexico and either remaining independent or seeking the protection of some power. A controversy has arisen as to whether or not this discussion actually took place. Bancroft, Calif., V, 59-63, supports the negative, but in so doing he quotes various people, including Vallejo, Alvarado, Revere, who state that the subject was discussed. Smith, op.cit., I, 329, 526, and McKittrick, op. cit., pp. 248-252 both believe that the matter was taken up. Supposedly Pico, Spence, and Hartnell spoke for England, certain others for France, and Vallejo for the United States. The story goes that Vallejo seeing that he was outnumbered by the opposition, which would undoubtedly unite in favor of England, withdrew with his adherents, thus leaving the junta without a quorum and preventing European

originated among the supporters of the United States. On June 13, 1846 he wrote to Bankhead, "I have little doubt that I shall find the object of that power /the United States/ will be obtained, either by voluntary subjection on the part of the Inhabitants, or by the United States having taken possession of the Principal Port, in consequence of the recent hostilities with Mexico."[46] Thus the Admiral was not greatly surprised when he found, upon his arrival in California, the flag of the United States flying over Monterey.

On the same day Seymour wrote to the Admiralty.

I have not, after the reports made by Captain Gordon and others to me, of the state of affairs on that coast, judged it advisable to proceed there, under the views expressed by the Earl of Aberdeen to Her Majesty's Minister in Mexico, deprecating interference, while California formed a part of the Mexican Republic. I however (as I have already reported) sent the Juno to Monterey and San Francisco on the 11th of May, with instructions to ascertain the Security of British Subjects, and observe what was passing.

I also directed Captain Blake, in the event of California declaring or having declared its independence of Mexico to use any influence he could obtain to counteract any inclination on the part of those in Authority to place themselves under the Exclusive Control or Protection of any Foreign Powers, without the participation of Great Britain; and gave him copies of Lord Aberdeen's Letters, (which I had procured since my arrival on this Coast) of the 31st of December, 1844 to Mr. Bankhead and the Consul at Tepic, of the same date, for his information.

This contingency having occurred while I remain on the Coast, I deem it right, although I can form no very favorable anticipation of a satisfactory result, to proceed to Monterey, and ascertain the actual state of affairs; and it is my intention to sail from San Blas, for that purpose this evening.[47]

This then is the reason that Seymour sailed for Monterey -- a voyage which contemporaries and many historians considered a "naval race" with

---

45. Cont'd from Page 90: - intervention.
    The junta at Monterey was controlled by the party of Jose Castro, one of two rival factions in California. The proposed meeting at Santa Barbara, of which Seymour had heard, was called by Pio Pico, the leader of the other faction, as a counter measure. Governor Pico was also the leader of the supporters of England. (See Smith, op. cit., I, 338 and Bancroft, Calif., V, 74-75.) Although the Santa Barbara meeting was never held, it is probable that it was called, in part at least, to discuss the political future of California. Bancroft, Calif., V, 47, 65-71.
    46. Adams, op. cit., p. 257.
    47. Ibid., p. 258.

Commodore Sloat for the seizure of California. Seymour's action was essentially negative, in line with Aberdeen's passive policy, carried out with little hope of success, instead of the dynamic plan of conquest that Americans apparently believed it to be. It may be true that Seymour personally was interested in seeing England acquire California.

> Nevertheless, neither he nor any other British agent felt free to undertake active operations to secure California to Great Britain, and all that can be said is that they were hoping for some fortunate chance that might permit them to forestall American plans while yet they maintained the purely passive attitude directed by Aberdeen.[48]

In summing up England's attitude toward California, it might be said that British agents were genuinely interested in securing California for Great Britain but that their efforts were made without instructions from their government and were either checked or reproved by it.

The lack of interest displayed by the government was probably caused by a variety of reasons, among which were a hostile attitude toward any colonial expansion, insufficient information about California, difficult relations with Mexico, and the complexities of the Texas situation. The only break in her complete indifference toward California was manifest in Aberdeen's despatch of December 31, 1844. That break was only temporary, and even so the instructions which it prompted were so passive that British representatives in the New World were convinced that no beneficial results could be obtained. "The theory of an active British governmental design upon California is then wholly without foundation."[49]

The negativistic policy of Aberdeen and Palmerson in regard to California was upheld by Parliament. In 1845 the French newspaper _Presse_ reported that after the fall of Santa Anna, documents pertaining to a proposed cession of California to Great Britain for 25,000,000 piastres had been found among his papers.[50] In response to questioning on this subject in the House of Commons on March 7, 1845, Sir Robert Peel styled the report as "utterly without foundation", and Palmerston, for the previous government, made similar denials.[51] There was no further discussion of the issue at this time. In August, 1846, when the Mexican War was in progress, the government was criticised by Bentinck and Disraeli for failure to protect the interests of British merchants and bondholders in Mexico and California. However, the policy of Palmerston, who was again

---

48. Adams, op. cit., p. 259.
49. Ibid., p. 264.
50. A similar report was made by Wilson Shannon, U.S. Minister to Mexico, to Calhoun, Secretary of State, on January 9, 1845. Manning, Dip. Corres., VIII, 695.
51. Hansard's Parliamentary Debates (London), LXXVIII, 430-431. This incident was reported by Edward Everett, U.S. Minister to Great Britain, to the Secretary of State in his despatch of March 28, 1845. Manning, Dip. Corres., VII, 265.

in office, was upheld by other members of Parliament.[52]

3. PARTISANS OF GREAT BRITAIN IN CALIFORNIA

Within California there was a large number of people who favored the English cause, after it became apparent that Mexican rule was unsatisfactory. The state of anarchy existing in California in the 1830's and 1840's led most of the substantial citizens to seek a more stable form of government. The most acceptable solutions proposed were California independence, annexation to the United States, a British protectorate, or a French protectorate.

The faction which favored a British protectorate offered most of the advantages held out by the American party, such as a strong, stable government and relatively free institutions, and yet was not hampered by the objections attached to the partisans of the United States. The participation of American citizens in California revolts had excited fear and suspicion, and the Mexican description of the events in Texas had been unfavorable to them. The actions of rough American frontiersmen and the brusque, overbearing, strenuous ways of American settlers also alarmed the easy going Californians.

As a result many of the most prominent citizens, especially in the south, favored Great Britain.[53] The pro-British party naturally included nearly all of the men of British birth, the most active of whom were Forbes, Spence, and Dr. James Stokes.[54] It also included many of the native California leaders; those who had approached Forbes in 1844 with a plan for a British protectorate. Micheltorena had expressed himself to Hartnell as being friendly to the British party. And in 1846, as decisive action approached, the British party was led by Governor Pico and probably included such men as Jose Castro, Pablo de la Guerra, and Juan Alvarado, who sided with England mainly to keep their country out of the hands of the United States.[55] However, to the British supporters Forbes could give no encouragement, but could only advise them not to accept the control of any other nation, should California become free. At the same time the American party was growing stronger, bolstered up by the support of the overland immigrants who were anxious to see California a part of the United States.

4. AMERICAN FEAR OF BRITISH AGGRESSION IN CALIFORNIA

In spite of the official indifference of Breat Britain towards California, the American public, the American press, and many American officials were apprehensive lest this province should be taken by Great

---

52. Hansard's Parliamentary Debates, LXXXVIII, 978-995.
53. Smith, op. cit., I, 327-328.
54. Bancroft, Calif., V, 68-72.
55. Smith, op. cit., I, 328-329; Bancroft, Calif., V, 69.

Britain before the United States could act.[56] American apprehension was based on rumors, conjectures, and the activities of British agents, who, as we have seen, were striving to interest their government in some plan of acquisition. In addition, neither the American public nor the American government was, of course, aware of the official British attitude on this subject.

Bancroft states that beginning in 1836 there were frequent rumors of foreign interference in the form of conquest, protectorates, or annexation. The first report of such a step in American diplomatic correspondence were made in 1837 when W. D. Jones wrote to John Forsyth, the Secretary of State, that a plan, sponsored by General Michelena, was on foot to sell Texas and California to the British government at the rate of twenty-five cents per acre to pay off the Mexican debt. "If that can't be effected, to dispose of it, to an English company, to colonize, to arrest the ambitious views, of the United States, whose policy, is to possess themselves, of that fine country, this government asserts..."[57] On March 8, 1838 Jones also reported the passage of a law by the Mexican Congress which authorized the sale of lands in California, Chihuahua, New Mexico, Sonora, and Texas exclusively to British subjects.[58]

Alexander Forbes' California, which contained the first proposal for the transfer of California to Great Britain in payment for the Mexican debt, stirred up considerable alarm in the United States.[59]

The next repercussion of American fears was Commodore Jones' seizure of Monterey in 1842. While lying at Callao he received a report that war between the United States and Mexico was imminent and fearing British designs on California, Jones sailed for Monterey to prevent the British fleet from occupying California.[60] It has been shown that his suspicions were unfounded.

In Mexico City the United States Minister, Waddy Thompson, was giving vent to his fears of British aggression. In his despatches to Daniel Webster, Secretary of State at this time, Thompson advocated taking California because of its natural worth and because of the danger of it falling into the hands of Great Britain.[61] Webster, however, deprecated

---

56. The best study of this subject is found in Robert Glass Cleland, The Early Sentiment for the Annexation of California: An Account of the Growth of American Interest in California from 1835 to 1846, Reprinted from the Southwestern Historical Quarterly, XVIII, Nos. 1, 2, and 3. (Austin, Texas, 1915), pp. 82-83.
57. Jones to Forsyth, Mexico City, April 17, 1837 and idem to idem, April 26, 1837, Manning, Dip. Corres., VIII, 418-419.
58. Idem to idem, March 8, 1838, Manning, Dip. Corres., VIII, 428.
59. Cleland, Early Sentiment, pp. 82-83; Engelson, "Proposals," loc. cit., XVIII, 139.
60. Davis, op. cit., pp. 115-116; Bancroft, Calif., IV, 298-314.
61. Thompson to Webster, April 29, 1842, Manning, Dip. Corres. VIII, 480-485; Idem to idem, Ibid., VIII, 511; Thompson to Upshur, October 14, 1843, Ibid., VIII, 564.

such fears.[62] But other American agents in Mexico were similarly apprehensive. Duff Green reported that an English mortgage on California for $26,000,000 would expire in 1847 and unless paid before that time would result in the transfer of that territory to Great Britain.[63] Wrote Charles A. Wickliffe, Special Agent of the United States to Texas, to the Secretary of State, "Look well to one probable result if Mexico declares war, -- Before the fact is known she will have transferred to England California & the Bay of San Francisco."[64] The report that Santa Anna's papers revealed negotiations for the sale of California was duly reported to Washington by the United States Minister to Mexico.[65] William S. Parrott, confidential agent of the United States in Mexico, reported that Great Britain had increased her fleet in the Pacific with the rumored intention of seizing California in case of war between Mexico and the United States in order to protect the mortgage of British bondholders.[66] In August, 1846 Parrott reported MacNamara's imminent departure for California to carry out his colonization project.[67]

In the meantime Larkin had been calling his government's attention to the activities of the Hudson's Bay Company in California, as well as reporting rumors of British schemes to acquire that province.[68]

The Hudson's Bay Company, the supposed agent of British Imperialism, was not only carrying on a large trade with California and trapping in the interior, but was taking an open part in revolutionary outbreaks. On July 10, 1845, he reported that the English government was instigating a plan to send Mexican troops into California and that two English commercial houses had agreed to accept the expedition's drafts. He also reported that both an English vice-consul and a French consul were being supported by their respective governments, although there was no commercial reason for their being there.[69]

The press of the United States not only printed the facts, rumors, and conjectures that found their way into governmental correspondence but elaborated upon them and displayed considerable excitement over California.[70] "The importance of the question of foreign interference in California lies not so much, however, in its effects upon the popular

---

62. Cleland, Early Sentiment, pp. 84-85.
63. Ibid., p. 86.
64. Wickliffe to James Buchanan, April 3, 1845, Manning, Dip. Corres., XII, 421.
65. Wilson Shannon to John Calhoun, January 9, 1845, Ibid., VIII, 695.
66. Parrott to Buchanan, May 13, 1845, Ibid., VIII, 715-716.
67. Cleland, Early Sentiment, p. 89.
68. Larkin to Calhoun, Monterey, August 18, 1844, Manning, Dip. Corres., VIII, 639; Idem to idem, June 6, 1845, Ibid., VIII, 721-722; Idem to idem, April 17, 1846, Ibid., VIII, 841-842.
69. Larkin to Buchanan, July 10, 1845, Ibid., VIII, 735-736.
70. Bancroft, Calif., IV, 110, 260, 298; Cleland, Early Sentiment, pp. 92-93; Smith, op. cit., I, 323-324, 525-526.

mind as upon the policy pursued by the government."[71] From 1845 on the apprehension of the United States government of foreign aggression in California had a direct bearing on the administration's course of action.

The fear of foreign aggression was reflected in instructions, dated October 17, 1845, sent to Larkin when he was appointed confidential agent of the United States. The despatch stated that in order to protect Ammerican commercial interests Larkin "...should exert the greatest vigilance in discovering and defeating any attempt, which may be made by foreign governments to acquire a control over that country." While the United States will not forcibly intervene to separate California from Mexico or to extend American sovereignty over it, the President "...could not view with indifference the transfer of California to Great Britain or any other European Power." The colonization of this province by a foreign monarchy would be opposed to the best interest of the colonists, the United States, and the nation involved. "On the contrary, even Great Britain, by the acquisition of California, would sow the seed of future war and disaster for herself..." Consequently, Larkin is instructed to warn the people and the government of California of the dangers of foreign intervention. "Whilst I repeat that this Government does not, under existing circumstances, intend to interfere between Mexico and California, it would vigorously interpose to prevent the latter from becoming a British or French colony."[72]

The same fear was expressed the following month in the instructions to John Slidell, appointing him United States Minister to Mexico. Wrote Buchanan, "From information possessed by this Department, it is to be seriously apprehended that both Great Britain and France have designs upon California...You will endeavor to ascertain whether Mexico has any intention of ceding it to the one or the other power; and if any such design exists, you will exert all your energies to prevent an act which, if consummated, would be so fraught with danger to the best interest of the United States."[73]

The culmination of the United States government's fear of European acquisition of California was Polk's vigorous reaffirmation of the Monroe Doctrine in his first annual message to Congress on December 2, 1845. Both the wording of the message and Polk's private utterances indicate that his statement applied to California as well as to Oregon.[74]

When he wrote -- "the people of this continent alone have the right to decide their own destiny. Should any portion of

---

71. Cleland, Early Sentiment, p. 93.
72. Buchanan to Larkin, October 17, 1845, Manning, Dip. Corres., VIII, 169-170.
73. Buchanan to Slidell, November 10, 1845, Manning, Dip. Corres., VIII, 172-182.
74. Cleland, Early Sentiment, p. 96.

of them, constituting an independent state, propose to unite themselves with our confederacy, this will be a question for them and for us to determine without any foreign interference" -- Polk desired to warn England that the United States would brook no interference in case the program entrusted to Larkin in California was a success, and the inhabitants sought annexation to this country.

Similarly, when he announced that "no future European colony or dominion, shall with our consent, be planted or established on any part of the North American continent," he wished to announce clearly and distinctly to the British government that any attempt she might take to gain control of California would be opposed with arms if necessary by the United States.[75]

5. ACTIVITIES OF THE BRITISH VICE-CONSUL IN CALIFORNIA

Despite Larkin's alarm over the fact that a vice-consul was being maintained by Great Britain in California, the British vice-consulate was never a dynamic tool of British aggression. The suggestion of Forbes that a protectorate could be obtained with little difficulty was met by a very cool response from Aberdeen. As stated above Forbes realized that the passive policy laid down by the Foreign Secretary offered little hope of success, and he threw his support behind continued Mexican sovereignty.

Forbes was not again stirred to positive action until Fremont appeared on the coast in the winter of 1845-1846. On January 28, 1846 he addressed to Oliveria a protest against Fremont's presence "with soldiers" in California, stating that,

> ...in obedience to the commands of Her Majesty's Government, it is the duty of the Undersigned to state clearly and distinctly to this Departmental Government that while Great Britain does not pretend to interfere in the political affairs of California, she would view with much dissatisfaction, the establishment of a protectorate power over this country, by any other foreign nation.[76]

When Aberdeen learned of this protest, he disavowed Forbes' action and censured him for assuming the authority to make such a statement. It seems apparent that Great Britain had no grand design if this slight activity could be criticised by the Foreign Secretary. That such a legitimate and well deserved remonstrance should be repudiated adds more evidence of the disinterested position of the British government.[77]

---

75. Ibid., pp. 96-97.
76. Adams, op. cit., p. 251.
77. Ibid., p. 252.

This incident, in addition to the previously expressed indifference of the British government, was enough to dishearten Forbes. On June 1, 1846 Larkin reported to Washington that he had had a private conversation with Forbes in which the British vice-consul stated that his instructions were not to have anything to do with the politics of California. Forbes went on to say that he was convinced that California would belong to the United States as a result of immigration, if not "by other means". The interference of any other power would only make affairs worse by prolonging the state of uncertainty. Finally, he stated that if he were not in the employ of the British government, he would advise the Californians to seek the aid of the United States. [78]

Fremont, in spite of Forbes' protest, was given tacit permission to spend the winter in California as long as he kept away from the settlements on the coast. But the "Pathfinder" disregarded this limitation and marched his men into the Salinas Valley, a position which threatened Monterey. When Jose Castro, commandant of the district, and Manuel Castro, prefect, protested sharply against this breach of faith, Fremont moved to a strong military position on Gavilan Peak and defied the Californians.

As the only British representative in California, Forbes was advised of the situation and instructed to restrain any British citizens who might wish to take part in the uprising.

Sub Prefecture
of the 2d District.

I have on this date received from the Prefecture an official letter in which I am informed of the following facts.

The laws and integrity of the country are violated by the Captain of the Army of the United States, Don J. C. Fremont, with an armed force. Therefore it has been demanded by the Prefecture and the Commanding General, that he withdraw from the limits of the Department. He has disobeyed this and has placed his force in a hostile position, also hoisting the flag of his nation on a peak of the Sierra Gavilan, seeking to exercise arbitrarily a dominion over all the pueblos of the District.

In such circumstances as surround us, I have believed it my duty to place them in your knowledge, and pointing out the importance of your exerting your authority, to the end which concerns you; so that as Vice-Consul of Her Britannic Majesty you may cooperate to repress and avoid as far as possible that any of the subjects of Her Majesty may interfere against

---

78. Larkin to Buchanan, June 1, 1846. Maning, Dip. Corres., VIII, 858-859.

the cause of the country and the Mexican Nation, and meanwhile, that the business may be decided or terminated in whatever manner it may be deemed fitting by the Government.

Remaining then assured of your efficient cooperation as above indicated, I take the opportunity of reiterating my consideration and respect.

God and Liberty! San Francisco, March 11, 1846.

Francisco Guerrero
/Rubric/

To the Vice-Consul of Her Britannic Majesty
Don Diego A. Forbes[79]

From this time on the California leaders made a point of keeping Forbes abreast of political and military developments and filing with him copies of significant documents. This has led one historian to say, "This correspondence...proves...that the California leaders were filing with Vice-Consul Forbes carefully certified and translated documents covering all the principal events, with the design and intent of ultimately requesting the intervention of Great Britain, when the time should seem desirable."[80] So positive a conclusion is not justified by the facts,[81] but the California leaders were undoubtedly hoping for some support from Great Brittain.

General Castro a short time later wrote to Forbes telling of Fremont's withdrawal from Gavilan Peak and enclosing copies of two pertinent letters. The first, dated March 6, 1846, was from the United States consul, Larkin, to Diaz, the alcalde of Monterey, attempting to explain Fremont's action, although adding that, "Captain Fremont has his own instructions, and is not subject to this consulate."[82] Larkin goes on to say that he hopes that bloodshed can be avoided by a conference between the opposing leaders. The second enclosure was also from Larkin to Diaz and contained a translation of Fremont's despatch of March 9, 1846 to Larkin, which Diaz had requested. This despatch stated in part, "I am fortifying myself as well as possible with the intention that, if we are attacked unjustly, we will fight to the last extremity without giving way, in the confidence that our country will avenge our deaths."[83] The three documents referred to above are preserved as copied in the vice-consul's hand on his "blotter". Presumably the letters

---

79. E. A. Wiltsee, "The British Vice-Consul in California and Events of 1846," California Historical Society *Quarterly*, X (June, 1931), 102.

80. Wiltsee, loc. cit., 100. The following correspondence of the British vice-consulate is taken from this reference.

81. Wiltsee makes other statements in this paper which cannot be supported.

82. Wiltsee, "British Vice-Consul," loc. cit., X, 103.

83. Ibid., X, 103.

received were forwarded by Forbes to his superiors.

The next document that appears in Forbes' files is Castro's proclamation, dated March 13, 1846, to the people of California denouncing Fremont's aggressive acts. It is signed as a true copy by Pio Pico and was apparently sent to the vice-consul by him.

Three months later when Fremont had returned from his trip to the north and the Bear Flag Revolt was getting under way, Castro addressed a letter to the commanding officer of the American corvette of war Portsmouth, then in San Francisco Bay, asking for an explanation of Fremont's behavior in invading the country, taking possession of the plaza of Sonoma, and seizing prominent Californians. This letter, dated June 17, 1846, the day before the Bear Flag Proclamation, and Lt. Montgomery's evasive reply, dated June 18, are copied on Forbes' blotter.

Next in order appears a letter from Governor Pico to Forbes enclosing a copy of Ide's "Bear Flag" proclamation of June 18, 1846, translated into Spanish by William E. Hartnell, the official translator, and certified by Pico's secretary, Jose Moreno. Pico's letter is a request for aid from Great Britain.

The undersigned, Constitutional Governor of the Department of the Californias, is sorry to inform Mr. Diego A. Forbes, Her Britannic Majesty's Vice Consul, that through the office of the Commander General of this Department and County Office of the Second District, he has been given the unpleasant news that a multitude of invaders from the United States of America have entered the northern part of the same Department, attacking four Mexican citizens, taking possession of the Sonoma garrison, and tearing the Mexican flag to pieces.

The undersigned has not had confirmed news that there has been an open declaration of war with that power; therefore, he resents strongly the audacious infamy perpetuated by the American foreigners, who, violating the sacred pacts and institutions of our Nation and ignoring all the gratitude which they should show for the hospitality they have received, in the most atrocious manner are trying to have this section of the Republic of Mexico present as sad a picture as the Department of Texas, practically consummating another great theft.....

The undersigned is satisfied that Great Britain, being an ally of the Republic of Mexico and both nations having great consideration for each other, in view of such an outrage, will doubtless give her protection. This inspires the undersigned to solicit help in the name of the Mexican Departmental Government through that consulate, as there is on the coast a war corvette, in the hope that this will be enough to stop the progress of the ambitions of the Americans.

The undersigned feels that this step taken to save his country will be approved by the Supreme National Authority, and consequently, believes that this petition will be granted.

In addressing this note to Mr. Diego A. Forbes, Her Britannic Majesty's Vice Consul, the undersigned requests that it will be given a quick solution and has the honor to offer him his high esteem and consideration.

God and Liberty, Santa Barbara, June 29, 1846, at 1 A.M.

Pio Pico
/Rubric/

Mr. Vice Consul of Her Britannic Majesty
Don Diego A. Forbes[84]

This letter was apparently forwarded to Admiral Seymour for action. On July 29, 1846 Pico addressed to Forbes an acknowledgement for Seymour's despatch of July 23, 1846, which is believed to be a reply to Pico's request for assistance.

As the position of the Californians became hopeless, Jose Castro, when he was about to flee to Mexico, sent to Forbes on August 9, 1846, three more papers concerning the struggle. Castro requested that they be held as proof of his behavior "...in case of an unforeseen disaster of war which might tend to blemish my reputation." The enclosures were (1) a copy of Commodore Stockton's letter of August 7, 1846, stating that no armistice was possible unless California declared her independence under the protection of the United States, (2) a copy of Castro's reply refusing to meet these terms, (3) Castro's proclamation to the Californians on leaving for Sonora.

Whatever may have been the purpose of these documents, no help could be expected from Great Britain and none was received. The British vice-consulate and the British naval forces maintained a purely neutral role. Such a position was recomended to Forbes by Admiral Seymour as he was about to sail from California for the Hawaiian Islands.

H. M. Ship Collingwood
Monterey, 22nd. July 1846

Sir,

On quitting the Coast of Upper California, it may be useful to you that I should shortly state my views of your situation as Her Majesty's Vice Consul in that Province, under present circumstances.

The Squadron of the United States having taken forcible Possession of the Principal Ports, in consequence of hostilities

---

84. Wiltsee, "British Vice Consul," loc. cit., X, 114-115.

having occurred on the Rio Grande between the Armies of the United States and Mexico, the value of the services of the Consuls of the different powers is enhanced, in order that they may assist in affording or obtaining Protection for their fellow subjects, whose interests may be compromised in the distracted State of Affairs which exists, or may be expected to prevail; I am, therefore, glad to have been informed by the Commodore Commanding the United States Squadron that there is no intention to disturb the Foreign Consuls in the exercise of their function.

I observe in the Proclamation issued on the 7th of July, that He acquaints the inhabitants that California will henceforward be a portion of the United States.

Whatever may be the expectations of that Officer, I apprehend He would not be warranted by the practice or Law of Nations, nor, I believe, by the Constitution of the United States, to declare that California has been annexed to that Republic; and that the Tenure under which the Forces of the United States at present hold this province should, therefore, be regarded as a provisional occupation pending future decisions, on the issue of the contest between the United States and Mexico; and in that light alone it should be regarded by you, until you receive instructions from the Department under which you act, for your conduct.

I recommend to you the stricted Neutrality between contending Parties, and to conduct yourself with the prudence and circumspection which are so essential to make your Services as Her Majesty's Vice Consul beneficial in the present State of Upper California.

I have the honor to be, Sir, your obedient servant,

G. F. Seymour
Rear Admiral and Commander in Chief

To
James Alexr. Forbes, Esqr.
Her Majesty's Vice Consul in California[85]

However, Forbes had already had sufficient proof of the British governments negative position to keep him from taking any aggressive action. As far as is known he took no further part in the affairs of 1846.

---

85. Wiltsee, "British Vice Consul," loc. cit., X, 118-119.

5. BRITISH VIEW OF THE AMERICAN CONQUEST

The war which resulted in American annexation of California was viewed in British eyes as one primarily concerned with Texas. In the pre-war years English diplomacy in North America had been active in regard to Texas, and the British view of California was subordinated to and conditioned by the Texas question. That Great Britain would not give assistance to Mexico in case of war with the United States, although she had endeavored to strengthen Mexico and prevent the annexation of Texas and California by the American Union, was an established element of British foreign policy.[86] American victories and Mexican ineptitude in waging war, and even in achieving national solidarity, made British neutrality more certain.[87]

At the outbreak of hostilities Lord Aberdeen expressed his opinion to the American minister that annexation of territory as a result of the war would be undesirable. To this statement McLane made the unmistakably equivocal reply that "...it was at present not easy to foresee all the consequences of a war which Mexico had so wantonly provoked, and in which the United States had so much injustice and so many wrongs to redress."[88] The cause of the United States was extremely unpopular in Great Britain in the early months of the war.[89] Polk's Annual Message of December 8, 1846, indicating that we intended to retain California, provoked a hostile response from the British press.[90] However, American victories, in addition to commercial advantages experienced by British merchants from United States control of Mexico and expected from its annexation of parts of Mexico, induced the British government to acknowledge American rights of conquest.[91] In his despatch of June 3, 1847, the United States minister in London wrote that he felt safe "...in saying that the Ministry is prepared to see the peace with Mexico made upon almost any terms that our conquests and our moderation may prescribe."[92] He also reported that England was "...preparing to hear of our negotiating for half, or two thirds, or even the whole of Mexico,"[93] and Lord Palmerston indicated that the United States might

---

86. Adams, op. cit., pp. 224-225.

87. Smith, op. cit., II, 305-306.

88. Louis McLane to James Buchanan, May 29, 1846, Manning, Dip. Corres., VII, 275.

89. Idem to idem, June 3, 1846, Ibid., VII, 276.

90. James D. Richardson, A Compilation of the Messages and Papers of the Presidents 1789-1891 (Washington, 1899), IV, 492-494. George Bancroft to James Buchanan, Jan. 4, 1847, Manning, Dip. Corres., VII, 289. Smith, Texas, II, 308.

91. Bancroft to Buchanan, Jan. 4, 1847, Manning, Dip. Corres., VII, 290. James McHenry Boyd, U. S. Charge d'affaires ad interim to Buchanan, Sept. 18, 1846, Ibid., VII, 289, Bancroft to Buchanan, June, 1847, Ibid., VII, 292. Smith, Texas, II, 303.

92. Bancroft to Buchanan, June 3, 1847, Ibid., VII, 292.

93. Smith, Texas, II, 309.

as well take all of Mexico.[94] When the Treaty of Guadalupe Hidalgo was received in England, attention had been diverted from the American scene to the revolutionary outbreaks enflaming all of Europe. What reaction there was expressed surprise at the moderation of the demands made by the United States rather than a feeling of hostility toward that state.[95]

94. Ibid.
95. Ibid.

EPILOGUE

The discovery of gold in 1849 fostered a world-wide interest in California and precipitated an unprecedented migration to the gold fields. In this migration British citizens played a role second only to that of American citizens. The British interest in the Gold Rush is indicated by the number of guidebooks to California published in the British Isles in that year as well as by frequent references to the gold regions in British periodicals.[1]

Beginning a short time later there appeared in the London bookstores published journals and reminiscences of various '49ers. A scoop for this type of literature was achieved by the publication in 1849 of a volume entitled Four Months among the Gold Finders in Alta California: Being the Diary of an Expedition from San Francisco to the Gold Districts.[2] Its author bore the improbable name of J. Tyrwhitt Brooks, M.D. This book met a phenomenal reception, being reviewed in most of the leading journals: the Times gave it nearly three columns, the Quarterly Review joined in its praise, and the Athenaeum devoted six columns to the book.[3] It was translated into several foreign languages and reprinted in America. The actual author was Henry Vizetelly,

---

1. David T. Ansted, The Gold Seeker's Manual, (London, 1849). William Thurston, Guide to the Gold Regions of Upper California (London, 1849). James Wyld, A Guide to the Gold Country of California. An Authentic and Descriptive Narrative of the Latest Discoveries in that Country, comp. from the Official Despatches of Colonel Mason, Lieutenant-Colonel Fremont, and Other Government Authorities...(London, 1849). The Gold Regions of California, Describing the Geography, Topography, History and General Features of that Country, From the Official Reports Transmitted to the American Government by Colonel Mason, Lieutenant-Colonel Fremont, Brigadier-General Jones, Lieutenant Emory, J. S. Folsom, Esq., ...(London, 1849). Guide to California. (With a Map) Containing an account of the Climate, Soil and Natural Productions of Upper California, With Authentic Particulars Respecting the Gold Region, Derived from the Official Documents of the Government of the United States; also, a Complete Description of the Various Routes, and all Other Information Useful to Intending Emigrants (London, 1849). See references in Punch, XVIII (1849), p. 93, 104, 232, 233;XIX (1850), 102. Athenaeum (1849), 34, 116, 352, 510, 741, 766, 878, 1019, 1337. The Gentleman's Magazine, (Feb. - May, 1849), p. 192, 529; XXXIII (March, 1850), p. 307.
2. J. Tyrwhitt Brooks, Four Months among the Gold Finders in Alta California: Being the Diary of an Expedition from San Francisco to the Gold Districts (London, 1849).
3. Henry Vizetelly, Glances Back Through Seventy Years: Autobiographical and Other Reminiscences (2 vols., London, 1893), I, 343-347.

printer, publisher, journalist, and bon vivant, a man who had never been to California. The forgery's rapid acceptance indicates the cleverness of the author, the English interest in California, and the quantity of information available in England that would enable the author, not only to fool the public, but to produce a forgery which would be accepted by an authority such as Bancroft writing nearly thirty years later.[4]

More authentic records of experiences began to appear in 1850. The English reading public was able to choose from such titles as Adventures of a Gold Finder, written by Myself; Sights in the Gold Region, and Scenes by the way Personal Adventures in Upper and Lower California in 1848-9: with the Author's Experiences at the Mines: Golden Dreams and Waking Realities; Being the Adventures of a Gold Seeker in California and the Pacific Islands; An Excursion to California Over the Prairies, Rocky Mountains, and Great Sierra Nevada, with a Stroll Through the Diggings and Ranches of the Country; California: Its Gold and Its Inhabitants. Two of the better known works on the Gold Rush were brought out by Britishers a short time later. In 1855 Frank Marryat published his Mountains and Molehills; or Recollections of a Burnt Journal and J. D. Borthwick's Three Years in California appeared two years later.

The migration which this literature sought to direct, and did record, is indicated by the Census of 1850, in which, for the first time, the territories of the Pacific Coast were included. The numbers of immigrants from the British isles are as follows: England, 3050; Scotland, 883; Wales, 182; and Ireland, 2452, in all totalling more than the sum of immigrants from Germany and France, the birthplaces of the next largest numbers.[5] The figures given, however, are not complete as the results from San Francisco County were burned and those from Santa Clara and Contra Costa Counties were lost on the way to the Census Office.[6]

In 1849 a constitutional convention met at Monterey to establish a representative government for the new territory. A few men of British birth took part, although in numbers they were quite naturally overshadowed by both the Americans and the native Californians of Spanish extraction.

---

4. This historian accepts Dr. Brooks as a true California pioneer and writes "...the author's observations /are/ such as command respect." Bancroft, Calif., VI, 98n.

5. J. D. B. DeBow, The Seventh Census of the United States: 1850. Embracing a Statistical View of Each of the States and Territories... (Washington, 1853), p. xxxvii.

6. Ibid., p. 966.

It was in part because of the non-English speaking members that Hartnell was appointed interpreter and translator for the convention.[7] Several of the Spanish delegates spoke only through him, and he translated the constitution into Spanish for the benefit of the native Californians when it was submitted to the people for ratification on October 9, 1849.[8]

The reporter of the convention, John Ross Browne, was of Irish birth. A recent arrival in California, he was pressed into service because he was the only qualified stenographer in the area.[9] The debates in the convention were published under his name.[10]

Turning to members of the convention, Louis Dent, an Englishman, served as a delegate from Santa Barbara; Hugo Reid representated San Gabriel; and William E. Shannon, of Irish birth, was a delegate from Sacramento.[11] It is interesting to note that it was Shannon who proposed the free soil clause, which was adopted almost without discussion by the Californians but which was due to raise bitter opposition in the South and shake the Union to its foundations before the Compromise of 1850 sealed over the lengthening cracks and momentarily hid them from view.

The participation of these men in the constitutional convention marks a fitting close to the existence of the British pioneers as a separate national group in California. The American Republic, a kindred land to their own country, replaced Mexican rule. The convention now marked the extension of freely organized, representative government, the great contribution of the Anglo-Saxon Motherland, to California and the world. Under the American system thereby established, the British immigrants were effortlessly absorbed by the Americanized community, and the British pioneers became United States citizens.

---

7. John Ross Browne, Report of the Debates in the Convention of California, on the Formation of the State Constitution, in September and October, 1849 (Washington, 1849), p. 10.
8. Constitucion del Estado de California (San Francisco, 1849).
9. Francis John Rock, J. Ross Browne: A Biography (Washington, 1929).
10. Browne, op.cit.
11. Rockwell Dennis Hunt, The Genesis of California's First Constitution (1846-49) (Baltimore, 1895), p. 39. Cardinal Goodwin, The Establishment of State Government in California (New York, 1914), p. 84.

APPENDIX I

British ships engaging in trade along the California coast. Ships that remained from one year to the next are listed under both years.

1822   Colonel Young, Snipe, Lady Blackwood, John Begg, Claudine, Hawaii, Sir Francis Baring.

1823   John Begg, Thomas Nowlan, Neptune, Hebe.

1824   Hawaii, Young Tartar, Pizarro, Royal George.

1825   Young Tartar, Bengal, Eliza, Merope, Pizarro, Junius, Inca.

1826   Thomas Nowlan, Young Tartar, Eliza, Inca, Olive Branch, Pizarro, Solitude, Speedy.

1827   Cadboro, Fulham, Huascar, Olive Branch, Solitude, Thomas Nowlan, Young Tartar.

1828   Fulham, Funchal, Huascar, Solitude, Thomas Nowlan, Vulture.

1829   Ann, Funchal, Indian, James Coleman, Susana, Thomas Nowlan, Vulture.

1830   Ayacucho, Dryad, Funchal, Jura, Seringapatan, Thomas Nowlan.

1831   Ayacucho, Dryad, Eliza.

1832   Ayacucho, Seringapatan.

1833   Ayacucho, Charles Eyes.

1834   Ayacucho, Bonanze, Llama, Tansuero.

1835   Ayacucho, Clementine.

1836   Ayacucho, Clementine.

1837   Ayacucho, Cadboro, Clementine, Llama.

1838   Ayacucho, Cadboro, Columbian, Fearnaught, Flibbertygibbett, Index, Llama, Nereid.

1839   Ayacucho, Clementine, Flibbertygibbett, Index.

1840   Ayacucho, Columbia, Fly, Forager, Index.

1841   Ayacucho, Columbia, Cowlitz, Index, Rosalind.

1842   Cowlitz, Index, Rosalind, Valleyfield.

1843   Cowlitz, Index, Valleyfield, Vancouver.

1844   Brothers.

1845   Cowlitz, Star of the West, Vancouver.

APPENDIX II

List of British grantees compiled from <u>Jimeno's and Hartnell's Indexes</u> <u>of Land Concessions.</u>

Date	Rancho	Grantee
May 17 '36	Canada de Tamales	Jaime Ricardo Berey (James R. Berry)
Aug 29 '35	Cueros del Benado	Juan Ma. Marron
Aug 29 '39	Sausalito	Juan Read
Jun 28 '34	Los Carneros	David Letajon (David Littlejohn)
Apl 15 '39	Encinal	David Spence
Jul 28 '35	Sausalito	Guillermo Richardson
Apl 10 '39	Las Pocitas	J. Noriega y Robto Livermot (Robert Livermore)
Aug 21 '39	S. Pedro y San Pablo	Diego Forbes (James Alexander Forbes)
Sep. 4 '39	Estero Americano	Eduardo Ml. Mackintosh
Jun 8 '39	Tamalas	Jose Snook (Joseph F. Snook)
Oct 16 '39	Corte de Madero	Juan Martin
Nov 2 '40	Chisino	Marcos West (William Mark West)
Aug 4 '40	Canada de Reymundo	Juan Coopinger (John Coppinger)
Mar 14 '41	Carne Humana	Eduardo A. Bale
Apl 16 '41	Santa Anita	Perfecto Hugo Rid (Hugo Reid)
Aug 28 '41	Tudos Stcs. y Santo	Guillermo Hartnell
Feb 24 '36	Terreno inmedto. al de Sta. Rosa	Juan Cooper
Feb 16 '42	San Bernardo	Franco Snook (Joseph F. Snook)
Apl 29 '42	Tinacac	Guilmo. Domgo. Foxon (Benjamin Foxen)
Aug 10 '42	Agua Hedionda	J. Ma Marron
Apl 30 '40	Los Dos Pueblos	Nicolas A. Den
Oct 23 '43	Rio de Jesus Ma.	Thomas Hardy
Feb 20 '44	Las Juntas	Guillermo Wehl (William Welsh)
Feb 14 '44	San Pedro y Gallis	Timoteo Morfil (Timothy Murphy)
Feb 28 '44	Rio de Monterey	Thomas Cole
Feb 29 '44	Potrero de Sta. Clara	Diego Forbes
Jun 17 '44	Coyollomi	Roberto Tomas Riley (Robert T. Ridley)
Nov 18 '44	Rio Sacramto	Guillermo Dickey
Nov 3 '44	(11 square leagues on the Cosumnes)	Guillo. Edo Hartnell
Mar 27 '45	En la Mision de San Gabriel	Miguel Ma. Blanco (Michael White)
Mar 31 '45	Santa Anita	Perfecto Hugo Reid
Apl 5 '45	Potreros de la Sierra del Agua Caliente (San Juan Capo)	Juan Foster (John Forster)
May 26 '45	Terreno de San Gabriel	Henrique Dalton
Sep 24 '45	Canada de los Osos, Pecho e Yslai	Jas. Scott y John Wilson
Oct 10 '45	Canada del Chorro (S.L.s Obo)	Scott y Wilson

Date	Rancho	Grantee
Dec 11 '45	Rancho Nacional Diego	San Juan Foster
Feb 5 '46	Jonive (Sonoma)	Santiago Black
Apl 29 '43	Muscupiavit	Miguel Blanco (Michael White)
Mar 22 '43	San Jacinto y San Borgonio	Santiago Johnson
Jul 22 '45	La Puente de San Gabriel	Juan Roland y Julian Workman (John Rowland and William Workman)
Jun 16 '46	Milcuatay	A.J.B. Martin y J. B. Buet

BIBLIOGRAPHY

1. BIBLIOGRAPHY.

    Cowan, Robert Ernest. A Bibliography of the History of California,
        1510-1930. 3 vols. J. H. Nash, San Francisco, 1933.

        In spite of some omissions and incomplete annotation, this
        bibliography is far ahead of any other of California history.

2. HISTORIES OF CALIFORNIA.

    Bancroft, Hubert Howe. History of California. 7 vols. The History
        Co., San Francisco, 1884-1890.

        Because of its sheer mass of detail, this work is valuable for
        almost any special study of California history. In some cases
        it serves as a depositary for source material. The Pioneer
        Index, an attempt to list and give some information about every
        person to come to California before 1848, was of special impor-
        tance in the composition of this thesis.

    Caughey, John Walton. California. Prentice-Hall, Inc., New York,
        1940.

        An excellent one-volume history, containing a valuable biblio-
        graphy.

    Chapman, Charles Edward. The Founding of Spanish California: The
        Northwestern Expansion of New Spain, 1687-1783. The MacMillan
        Co., New York, 1916.

        "It provides a new interpretation of the Spanish period of
        California history, treating it from the larger sphere of
        American history rather than as a local record, especially
        as concerns the struggle of Spain and the other nations for
        frontage on the Pacific Coast."

    _____. A History of California, The Spanish Period. The MacMillan
        Co., New York, 1921.

        This volume is considered by many to be the best history of
        the period prior to the American conquest. International
        phases are well covered, and the bibliography is especially
        good.

Cleland, Robert Glass. _From Wilderness to Empire, A History of California 1542-1900_. Alfred A. Knopf, New York, 1944.

A brief but accurate history of California, presented in an unusually readable style.

Forbes, Alexander. California: _A History of Upper and Lower California from their Discovery to the Present Time; Comprising an Account of the Climate, Soil, Natural Productions, Agriculture, Commerce &c_. John Henry Nash, San Francisco, 1937.

Originally published in 1839, this volume had for its purpose the promotion of an English protectorate over California. The author did not visit California until long after its publication.

Richman, Irving Berdine. _California Under Spain and Mexico 1535-1847_. Riverside Press, Cambridge, 1911.

Although not of first rank, this volume provides certain information, especially on international affairs, that could not be found elsewhere.

3. SPECIAL PHASES OF CALIFORNIA HISTORY.

Adams, Ephraim Douglas. _British Interests and Activities in Texas 1833-1846_ and "Addendum. English Interest in the Annexation of California." Johns Hopkins Press, Baltimore, 1910.

The addendum, based on the British archives, provides the principal published material on the official British attitude toward taking California.

Cleland, Robert Glass. _The Early Sentiment for the Annexation of California: An Account of the Growth of American Interest in California from 1835 to 1846_. Reprinted from the Southwestern Historical _Quarterly_, XVIII, Nos. 1, 2, and 3; Austin, Texas, 1915.

This is the definitive study of "manifest destiny" as applied to California.

——————————. _Pathfinders_. Powell Publishing Co., Los Angeles, 1929.

Pathfinders, as its name implies, is a book dealing with those who opened up the approaches to California. It is written in Dr. Cleland's usual scholarly yet interesting style.

Garrison, Myrtle. _Romance and History of California Ranchos._
Harr Wagner Publishing Co., San Francisco, 1935.

A brief history of the more important ranchos, this volume
is neither scientific in its research, nor accurate in its
details.

Hanna, Phil Townsend. _The Dictionary of California Land Names._
Automobile Club of Southern California, Los Angeles, 1946.

The origin of the name born by each geographical expression
and political division is given when that name can be traced.

Knowland, Joseph R. _California, A Landmark History. Story of the
Preservation and Marking of Early Day Shrines._ Tribune Press,
Oakland, California, 1941.

A record of landmarks restored and historic spots marked by
permanent monuments and tablets. Each landmark is briefly
described.

Odgen, Adele. _The California Sea Otter Trade 1784-1848._ University
of California Press, Berkeley and Los Angeles, 1941.

A complete and scholarly treatment of the entire sea otter
trade insofar as California is concerned. The author has
used the material available on this coast, as well as
official documents in Mexico City and Washington.

Smith, Justin H. _The War With Mexico._ 2 vols. The MacMillan Co.
New York, 1919.

This work, while primarily devoted to Texas, contains a valuable chapter and extensive footnotes, based on multi-
archival research, on foreign intrigues in California from
1836 to 1846.

4. SOCIAL AND CULTURAL LIFE IN CALIFORNIA.

Bancroft, Hubert Howe. _California Inter Pocula._ The History Co.,
San Francisco, 1888.

This volume consists of material left over from Bancroft's
History of California. It contains anecdotes, stories of
California, and observations on its society.

—————————° _California Pastoral 1769-1848_. The History Co., San Francisco, 1888.

The institutions and society of California's pastoral period are discussed topically.

Dakin, Susanna Bryant. _A Scotch Paisano: Hugo Reid's Life in California 1832-1852_. University of California Press, Berkeley, 1939.

A good biography of one of the British pioneers by a competent scholar.

Garner, Bess Adams. _Windows in an Old Adobe_. Progress-Bulletin, Pomona, California, 1939.

By writing of one early family, the author has provided a picture of California as a Mexican province.

Harding, George L. _Don Augustin V. Zamorano Statesman, Soldier, Craftsman, and California's First Printer_. The Zamorano Club, Los Angeles, 1934.

Zamorano was one of Mexican California's most versatile men and in this volume is well portrayed.

McKittrick, Myrtle M. _Vallejo Son of California_. Binfords and Mort, Portland, Oregon, 1944.

This outstanding biography was found useful for the British pioneers associated with Vallejo.

Powers, Laura Bride. _Old Monterey California's Adobe Capital_. San Carlos Press, San Francisco, 1934.

A book dealing with the customs and life of early California.

Sanchez, Nellie Van de Grift. _Spanish Arcadia_. Powell Publishing Co., Los Angeles, 1929.

A non-political history of California, portraying the customs character, society, education and everyday life of the early Californians.

5. HISTORIES OF POLITICAL SUBDIVISIONS OF CALIFORNIA.

Except where annotations are made, these volumes conform to the standard local history, giving a brief history of the section and laudatory biographies of the leading citizens.

Haley, William. The Centennial Year Book of Alameda County, California. William Haley, Oakland, 1876.

Hittell, John S. A History of the City of San Francisco and Incidentally of the State of California. A. L. Bancroft and Company, San Francisco, 1878.

A valuable and reasonably reliable history of San Francisco. Hittell's works are far superior to the typical county history.

O'Neill, Owen H. History of Santa Barbara County, State of California. Its People and Its Resources. Santa Barbara, 1939.

Sawyer, Eugene T. History of Santa Clara County with Biographical Sketches. Historic Record Company, Los Angeles, 1922.

Soule, Frank; Gihon, John H., M.D.; and Nisbet, James, The Annuals of San Francisco. D. Appleton and Company, New York, 1855.

Although this volume contains a few pages on San Francisco before the American conquest, it is most valuable for the early period under American rule.

History of Marin County, California Including Its Geography, Geology, Topography, and Climatography, etc. Alley, Bowen and Company, San Francisco, 1880.

History of Santa Clara County, California, Including Its Geography, Geology, Topography, Climatography and Description, etc. Alley, Bowen and Company, San Francisco, 1881.

An Illustrated History of Los Angeles County, California. Containing a History of Los Angeles County from the Earliest Period, etc. Lewis Publishing Company, Chicago, 1889.

An Illustrated History of Sonoma County, California. Containing a History of the County of Sonoma from the Earliest Period, etc. Lewis Publishing Company, Chicago, 1889.

A Memorial and Biographical History of Northern California. Lewis Publishing Company, Chicago, 1891.

6. JOURNALS, TRAVELS, AND REMINISCENCES.

Beaglehole, J. C. The Exploration of the Pacific. A. and C. Black
    Ltd., London, 1934.

This volume is valuable as a convenient guide to the early
voyages along the Pacific coast. It is especially useful
for the three voyages of Captain Cook.

Beechey, F. W. Narrative of a Voyage to the Pacific and Beering's
    /sic/ Strait, To Cooperate with the Polar Expeditions:
    Performed in His Majesty's Ship Blossom, under the command of
    Captain F. W. Beechey, R. N., F. R. S., F. R. A. S. and
    F. R. G. S., In the Years 1825, 26, 27, 28. Henry Colburn
    and Richard Bentley, 1831.

Says Bancroft, "...the observations published in the voyager's
(Beechey's) narrative were perhaps more evenly accurate and
satisfactory than those of any preceding navigator. Beechey
and his companions confined their remarks closely to actual
observations."

Belcher, Captain Sir Edward. Narrative of a Voyage Around the
    World, Performed in Her Majesty's Ship Sulphur, During the
    Years 1836-1842, Including Details of the Naval Operations
    in China, From December, 1840 to November, 1841. Henry
    Colburn, London, 1843.

In the official account of Captain Belcher's expedition, the
chapters on California give an interesting picture of the
province in the late thirties. Belcher feels that California
has changed for the worse in the interval between Beechey's
and his own voyages.

Bryant, Edwin. What I Saw in California, Being the Journal of a
    Tour by the Emigrant Route and South Pass of the Rocky
    Mountains, Across the Continent of North America, the Great
    Desert Basin, and Through California, in the Years 1846, 1847.
    Fine Arts Press, Santa Ana, California, 1936.

Bryant came overland in the Jacob and Bryant Party of 1846.
He gives a complete and well written account of the journey
and his experiences and observations in California before and
during the Revolution of 1846.

Cleveland, H. W. S. Voyages of a Merchant Navigator of the Days
    that are Past. Harper and Brothers, New York, 1886.

An excellent reference for the sea otter trade, including a
first-hand account of "the battle of San Diego."

Colton, Walter. Three Years in California. A. S. Barnes & Co.,
    New York, 1850.

    A witty record of the author's experiences as alcalde of
    Monterey and adventures during the Gold Rush.

Cook, James. The Three Voyages of Captain Cook Round the World.
    7 vols. Longman, Hurst, Rees, Orme, and Brown; London, 1821.

    Little comment is necessary on the first-hand account of
    Captain Cook's three epoch-making voyages. After Cook was
    killed on the third voyage, the narrative was continued by
    his successor in command of the expedition. The narration
    is matter-of-fact, but the events related are sufficiently
    exciting in themselves.

Dana, Richard Henry, Jr. Two Years Before the Mast. A Personal
    Narrative. Riverside Press, Cambridge, Mass. 1911.

    This most famous book on California contains a complete record
    of the hide and tallow trade, as well as shrewd observations
    on Mexican society in California.

Davis, William Heath. Seventy-Five Years in California. John
    Howell, San Francisco, 1929.

    A record of an American merchant in early California, contain-
    ing much valuable information on his Anglo-Saxon colleagues.

Dawson, Nicholas. California in '41; Texas in '51. Grabhorn Press,
    San Francisco, 1933.

    Dawson, an Arkansas school teacher, journeyed overland to
    California with the Bartleson-Bidwell Party in 1841. The
    book offers a good account of the overland trip and a brief
    record of the author's experiences in California, including
    a short time spent hunting sea otters.

Drake, Francis. The World Encompassed by Sir Francis Drake. London,
    1854.

    One of the two first-hand narratives of the "Famous Voyage,"
    written by the nephew of Sir Francis.

Edwards, Phillip Leget. California in 1837. The Diary of Phillip
    Leget Edwards. The Great Cattle Drive from California to
    Oregon in 1837. Grabhorn Press, San Francisco, 1932.

    A record of the first attempt to drive cattle from California
    to Oregon. A brief, factual account of his stay in California

is given.

Farnham, T. J. <u>Life, Adventures, and Travels in California.</u> Nafis and Cornish, New York, 1849.

Farnham gives a vivid picture of early California, being very critical of the natives. A large part of the book is devoted to the Graham affair, in which he took an active interest.

Griffin, John S. <u>A Doctor Comes to California. The Diary of John S. Griffin, Assistant Surgeon with Kearny's Dragoons, 1846-1847.</u> California Historical Society, San Francisco, 1933.

This book is valuable for its description of the southern route and as a historical record of Kearny's activities in the conquest of California.

Hakluyt, Richard. <u>The Voyages of the English Nation to America.</u> 4 vols. E. & G. Goldsmith, London, 1890.

The author of the portion describing Drake's "Famous Voyage" has not been positively identified, but it is generally accepted that he accompanied Drake. This and Francis Drake's account are the two principal sources for this voyage.

Lyman, Chester S. <u>Around the Horn to the Sandwich Islands and California 1843-1850. Being a Personal Record Kept by Chester S. Lyman.</u> Yale University Press, New Haven, 1924.

In diary form, the book gives valuable comments on some of the early residents of California and the customs of the country.

Mahr, August C. <u>The Visit of the "Rurik" to San Francisco in 1816.</u> Stanford University Press, Stanford University, 1932.

An account of the Russian exploring expedition led by von Kotzebue, which visited California in 1816.

de Mofras, Duflot. <u>Duflot de Mofras' Travels on the Pacific Coast.</u> 2 vols. Fine Arts Press, Santa Ana, California 1937.

de Mofras had been an attache of the French Embassy at Madrid. He was commissioned by the French minister of foreign affairs to visit and report on the Mexican, American, English and Russian outposts along the Pacific coast. This book offers a description of the country and its inhabitants compiled from the books that had been printed up until that time and from de Mofras' own observations.

Newmark, Harris. Sixty Years in Southern California 1853-1913 Containing the Reminiscences of Harris Newmark. The Nickerbocker Press, New York, 1926.

This volume was used only for those Britishers who lived in Southern California and whose life spans extended well into the American period.

Nuttall, Mrs. Zelia. (Translator and Editor.) New Light on Drake: A Collection of Documents Relating to his Voyage of Circumnavigation 1577-1580. Printed for the Hakluyt Society, London, 1914.

A great store of documents concerning Drake's "Famous Voyage", Spanish and Mexican, as well as English, are provided herein.

Phelps, William D. Fore and Aft; or Leaves from the Life of an Old Sailor By "Webfoot". Nichols and Hall, Boston, 1871.

Phelps commanded the Alert on a trip to California in the early forties. This was the ship on which Dana served during most of his "two years before the mast". Phelps gives a description of the hide and tallow trade and brief notes on the men that he encountered in California.

Rezanov, Nikolai Petrovich. The Rezanov Voyage to Nueva California in 1806. The Report of Count Nikolai Petrovich Rezanov of his Voyage to that Provincia of Nueva Espana from New Archangel. Thomas C. Russell, 1926.

Rezanov gives his account of the first successful attempt to break down the Spanish trade barriers surrounding California.

Robinson, Alfred. Life in California, Being a Residence of Several Years in That Territory. William Doxey, San Francisco, 1897.

Robinson, an American supercargo, settled down in California and married a native girl. He gives an excellent picture of the life of foreigners in Mexican California.

Ruschenberger, W. S. W. Narrative of a Voyage Round the World During the Years 1835, 36, and 37. 2 vols. Richard Bentley, London, 1838.

Ruschenberger was a surgeon on the USS Peacock when that ship made a diplomatic expedition around the world. Chapters XXI and XXII describe the visit of the ship to California made as the result of a letter from U. S. citizens in the Hawaiian Islands, charging that Americans in California were being unjustly treated.

Simpson, Sir George. Narrative of a Journey Round the World, During the Years 1841 and 1842. 2 vols. Henry Colburn, London, 1847.

Simpson, Governor in Chief of the Hudson's Bay Company's territories in North America, devotes many pages to his experiences in California. He also comments on the California settlements and their inhabitants. He is very critical of most of the province's men and institutions.

Vancouver, George. A Voyage of Discovery to the North Pacific Ocean, and Round the World; In which the Coast of Northwest America Has Been Carefully Examined and Accurately Surveyed. Undertaken by His Majesty's Command, Principally with a View to Ascertain the Existence of any Navigable Communication Between the North Pacific and North Atlantic Oceans; and Performed in the Years 1790, 1791, 1792, 1793, 1794 and 1795, in the Discovery Sloop of War, and Armed Tender Chatham under the Command of Captain George Vancouver. 6 vols. Printed for John Stockdale, London, 1801.

The parts of this work relating to California are described in the text of Chapter I.

Von Chamisso, Adelbert. A Sojourn at San Francisco Bay 1816. The Book Club of California, 1936.

Von Chamisso was the scientist of the Russian scientific expedition commanded by Von Kotzebue. His account of the Rurik's visit to San Francisco is the most complete of the three first-hand accounts.

Wagner, Henry R. Sir Francis Drake's Voyage Around the World: Its Aims and Achievements. John Howell, San Francisco, 1926.

Wagner, one of the foremost authorities on Drake's "Famous Voyage", arrives at a new interpretation of the whole expedition.

Wilkes, Charles. Narrative of the United States Exploring Expedition During the Years 1838, 1839, 1840, 1841, 1842. 5 vols. Philadelphia, 1850.

Besides a straightforward account of the expeditions' visit to California, some statistics of the commerce and production of California are given.

Works, John. Fur Brigade to the Bonaventura. John Works' California Expedition 1832-1833 for the Hudson's Bay Co. California Historical Society, San Francisco, 1945.

This is a journal of one expedition of the Umpqua Brigade, which the Hudson's Bay Company sent each year to trap the back country of California.

7. ARTICLES IN PERIODICALS.

"Benjamin Foxen's Great Service to United States." The Grizzly Bear, XLVII. (May, 1930), 46-48.

The Foxen warned Fremont of the Californians' plan to ambush him in Gaviota Pass and guided him over San Marcos Pass, written by one of Foxen's descendants.

Burns, T. P. "History of a Montgomery Street Lot in Yerba Buena." California Historical Society Quarterly, XI (Mar., 1932), 69-72.

The history of this piece of property, laid out by Richardson at the founding of the city, is traced up to the present time.

―――――――――――――.
"The Oldest Street in San Francisco." California Historical Society Quartarly, XIII (Sept., 1934), 235-239.

The History of the oldest street in San Francisco from the calle de la fundacion, as laid out by Richardson, to the Grant Street of today.

Engelson, Lester G. "Proposals for the Colonization of California by England in Connection with the Mexican Debt to British Bond-holders 1837-1846." California Historical Society Quarterly, XVIII (June, 1932), 136-148.

The Mexican debt to British bondholders, which played an important part in plans for acquisition of California by Great Britain, is given its fullest treatment in this article.

Goodwin, Cardinal, "Foreigners in California Before 1842-11." Overland, May, 1912, pp. 415-422.

No bibliography is given, but this material seems to be taken principally from Bancroft, History of California, and other standard reference books.

Gray, Theodore. "Hide and Tallow Trade in Alta California, under Spanish and Mexican Rule, to 1845, inclusive." The Grizzly Bear, XXI (July, 1917), 4, 5, 22.

The material for this paper has been taken from the standard reference books on California history.

"Khlebnikov's Memoirs of California translated from the Russian and
   edited (with a Biographical Sketch of the Author) by Anatole G.
   Mazour." Pacific Historical Review, IX (Sept., 1940), 307-336.

   Khlebnikov spent a good share of his life in the service of the
   Russian-American Company. He succeeded Baranov as chief of the
   company's possessions in America. He made several trips to
   California, and his Memoirs contain observations on the missions,
   trade, population, forts, settlements, etc.

Leader, Herman. "A Voyage from the Columbia to California in 1840
   from the Journal of Sir James Douglas." California Historical
   Society Quarterly, VIII (June, 1929), 97-115.

   Portions of Sir James Douglas' journal are included which cover
   his trip to California in 1840, a trip which led to the establishment of a Hudson's Bay Company post in Yerba Buena.

Lyman, G. D. "The Scalpel Under Three Flags in California."
   California Historical Society Quarterly, IV (June, 1925),
   142-213.

   This is a fairly accurate and complete record of the physicians
   in early California.

Manning, William Ray. "The Nootka Sound Controversy." American
   Historical Association Annual Report for the year 1904, pp.
   279-478.

   This is the definitive work on the Nootka Sound Controversy in
   both its American and European phases.

Ogden, Adele. "Boston Hide Droghers Along California Shores."
   California Historical Society Quarterly, VIII (June, 1929),
   289-305.

   The hide and tallow trade in operation.

_____.
"The Californias in Spain's Pacific Otter Trade, 1775-1795." Pacific
   Historical Review, I (December, 1932), 444-469.

   Most of this material is covered in more detail in the author's
   The California Sea Otter Trade 1784-1848.

_____.
"Havens for Whalers." The Grizzly Bear, LVIII (Jan., 1936), 3, 18,
   19.

   A brief article on whaling ships in California harbors, based primarily on log books of the whalers. The author states that this article is to be expanded into a more complete work on whaling in California.

"Hides and Tallow: McCullock, Hartnell and Company, 1822-1828." California Historical Society *Quarterly*, VI (Sept., 1927), 254-264.

A well-documented account of the first foreign company to enter the hide and tallow trade in California.

de Rojas, Lauro. "California in 1844 as Hartnell Saw It." California Historical Society *Quarterly*, XVII (Mar., 1938), 21-27.

W.E.P. Hartnell, a man of British birth living in Monterey, describes many phases of California life for the benefit of British bondholders seeking to acquire California.

Schaffer, Joseph. "Letters of Sir George Simpson, 1841-1843." *American Historical Review*, XIV, (October, 1908), 70-94.

Simpson, Governor General of the Hudson's Bay Company, on a trip around the world, sent back letters to the Company's headquarters in London intended for the eyes of the government. He urged Great Britain to take California.

Watson, D. S. "Report on the First House in Yerba Buena." California Historical Society *Quarterly*, XI (Mar., 1932), 73-78.

The controversy as to the founder of Yerba Buena and the builder of the first there is settled in favor of William A. Richardson.

Wiltsee, E. A. "The British Vice Consul in California and Events of 1846." California Historical Society *Quarterly*, X (June, 1931), 99-128.

This report, based on some interesting letters to and from the British vice consulate, contains conclusions which are not warranted by the facts and which are not in accord with the findings of Professor Adams in his search of the British Record Office.

"Yerba Buena Biographies: W. A. Richardson." California Historical Society *Quarterly*, XIV (Mar., 1935), 123-125.

A brief biography of Richardson containing little that is not found in Bancroft.

8. MISCELLANEOUS.

Bancroft, Hubert Howe. *History of the Northwest Coast*. 2 vols.
The History Co., San Francisco, 1886.

This work is another part of Bancroft's monumental history of
the West. Like the other sections of his history, it does not
provide a smooth, well-interpreted record of the section, but
it does offer a mass of details that would be difficult to find
elsewhere.

Bolton, Herbert E. *Drake's Plate of Brass, Evidence of His Visit to
California in 1579*. California Historical Society, San
Francisco, 1937.

A statement of the finding of this very important record and
its significance.

De Bow, J. D. B. *The Seventh Census of the United States: 1850.
Embracing a Statistical View of Each of the States and Territories...* Beverly Tucker, Washington, D. C., 1853.

This is the first census in which California was included.
Many figures on California as a result are incomplete.

Drake, Eugene (Ed.). *Jimeno's and Hartnell's Indexes of Land Concessions, From 1830 to 1846; Also, Toma de Razon, or Registry
of Titles, for 1844-45; Approvals of Land Grants by the
Territorial Deputation and Departmental Assembly of California,
from 1835 to 1846. And a list of Unclaimed Grants. Compiled
from the Spanish Archives in the U.S. Surveyor-General's Office*.

This is a semi-official record of the provisional land grants
made by the governors and the final approval of the deputation
for the years indicated.

Garrison, George P. *Diplomatic Correspondence of the Republic of
Texas.* Annual Report of the American Historical Association
for the Year 1907, vol. 2; 1908, vol. 2, parts 1 and 2.
Government Printing Office, Washington, D. C.

Hoffman, Odgen. *Reports of Land Cases Determined in the United
States District Court for the Northern District of California.
June Term, 1853 to June Term, 1858, Inclusive.* Numa Herbert,
San Francisco, 1862.

This volume is especially valuable for the appendix which contains a record of all the claims presented to the Board of
Claims and the results of the claims.

Manning, William R. _Diplomatic Correspondence of the United States._ _Inter-American Affairs._ _1831-1860._ 12 vols. Carnegie Endowment for International Peace, Washington, 1936.

The correspondence concerning California prior to its conquest by the United States comes under the correspondence with Mexico and with other nations about Mexico.

Stewart, George R., Jr. _Ordeal by Hunger._ _The Story of the Donner Party._ Henry Holt and Company, New York, 1936.

Perhaps the best book on the Donner Party.